Heavo, Heavo, Lash up and Stow

Memories

During my travels in the 'Andrew' every so often events jogged my memory of my childhood days in London's East End.

In Bombay, visits to the Docks at Custom House with old Grandad came flooding back. Seeing the *Queen Mary* in New York made me recall seeing this great ship off the Isle of Wight during a school holiday camp. Christmas carols in the Indian Ocean revived memories of 'We're knocking at the knocker, ringing at your bell, please spare a copper for singing up so well!' A New Yorker said to us, 'This is our front line city.' I smiled when I remembered the front line E13 of the 1940s.

Of course memories can play tricks on us all, and I ask my comrades and fellow travellers of the war years to accept my apologies if my memory has failed me on occasions!

Heavo, Heavo, Lash up and Stow

A memoir of an East Ender's war

——— Ken Kimberley ———

'I want you lot fell in outside in the rig of the day in 10 minutes!'

• MEMOIRS OF THE 20TH CENTURY •

from

The NOSTALGIA Collection

**For Joan and my mother
and for those who never came home**

'You're not in the Far East – you're in RNB Chatham, so get that white cap off!'

© Ken Kimberley and
Silver Link Publishing Ltd 1999

First published in December 1999

British Library Cataloguing in Publication Data

A catalogue record for this book is available from the British Library.

ISBN 1 85794 134 9

Silver Link Publishing Ltd
The Trundle
Ringstead Road
Great Addington
Kettering
Northamptonshire NN14 4BW

Tel/Fax: 01536 330588
email: sales@slinkp-p.demon.co.uk

Printed and bound in Great Britain

Contents

Introduction

Summer, 1931

It was a sunny Monday morning washday.

'Gran, Gran, what can I do?' I asked her.

She took the cover off the mangle that stood outside the scullery door and put the bowl of washing on the wooden table that stood beside it.

'Well,' she said, 'for a start you can turn the mangle handle for me.'

I grasped the handle with both hands and whizzed it around, watching the water squeeze out between the rollers.

'Not so fast, not so fast!' she said as she fed one of Grandad's Sunday-best shirts through the wooden rollers.

I helped her peg the washing out. She hoisted the clothes line high above the fence, and her washing flapped about in the breeze with everybody else's down the street.

'What can I do now Gran?'

'Well, if you hadn't buried all those soldiers out here in the yard that your Mum buys you, you could play with them. And what about the motor bus I bought you last week?'

'The wheels have dropped off,' I said.

'Oh, Grandad'll fix those for you when he comes home from work. I know,' she added. 'You can shell these peas for Grandad's dinner. Your Grandad likes a few peas with his cold meat and pickles.'

Pop, pop, pop went the pea pods as I emptied the fat juicy looking peas into Gran's colander. I looked at the empty pods that lay on the ground around me. 'They look like ships,' I thought.

'Gran, Granny, it's raining!'

She hurried through the scullery saying, 'Help me get the washing in.'

I did as she asked and at the same time filled my pockets with the empty pea pods.

'I'm going up to have forty winks,' she said. 'Open the door for Aunt Liz when she calls.'

'Yes Gran,' but I did have my thoughts on other things!

I reached up and turned on the tap that filled the sink in the scullery, emptied my pockets and floated my 'ships' on the water. I then helped myself to some matchsticks from the box that was always on the gas stove, and with one of Gran's meat skewers I made a hole in the middle of each pod. I took yesterday's *Daily Herald* off the copper, and with Gran's scissors cut out a tiny piece of the paper. I then threaded the match through the two holes I had made in the paper, and carefully put the 'mast' with its paper sail back into the pea pod.

With my finger I then gave each 'ship' a gentle shove, and stood back to admire my 'fleet' as it gently rocked its way around Gran's scullery sink. I looked through the parlour window to see if Aunt Liz was coming. All I could see were the big puddles in the road, and the rainwater that went gushing along down the gutters.

Soon the rain had stopped and the sky was blue again. Hurrying back into the scullery, I lifted some of my ships out of the sink, tip-toeing about because I didn't want to disturb Gran and her forty winks! I was careful to put the catch up on the front door, as I had seen her do, then, kneeling down on the pavement, I put my 'ships' into the water as it went rushing along the gutter. Before I could stand up, they were halfway down Khartoum Road.

'Kenny, Kenny, what are you doing down there?' Aunt Liz called out as I stood by the drain hole watching my 'fleet' disappear down it.

From that day on I loved ships (and trains, of course). Was it because my great grandfather had been a Channel pilot off Deal in Kent? My cousin, George Thompson, who also served in the Navy, has recorded with his painstakingly nurtured family tree that our Thompson forebears have been mariners since 1679. Billy Wilkins, another cousin, and lifelong pal, also preferred the Senior Service. The sea, it seems, has been in our blood for a very, very long time!

With my first fretwork set I made models of the *Golden Hind*, the *Santa Maria*, the *Mayflower* and so many others. Conventional stands were not for me. I floated each one on a sea of plaster of Paris, all painted to look like real waves, of course!

'Where's it going, Grandad?' we would ask when he took Bob and me down to the docks at Custom House to see off the big ships.

'Oh, all round the world,' he would say.

Up in bed later that night we would listen to the trams going up and over the sewer bridge down

Balaam Street, and far, far away a ship's siren sounded. I thought of Grandad's words, 'All round the world'. Gosh, I'd like to go all round the world!

'Do you think we'll ever go all round the world, Bobby?' I would ask him.

Winter, 1947

I walked up the gravel drive, as I had done so often with Bob in years gone by. Today it was strewn with weeds and ankle-deep in last autumn's leaves. Waist-high grass concealed the headstones, and the small chapel looked sad and neglected! 'To be expected,' I thought, 'after six long weary years of war.'

I followed the trampled-down grass that old Turner and his mate had made to Dad's grave. Gosh, what a transformation! Dad's grave looked now as I remembered it to be in my schooldays. 'All smart and shipshape' as old Taff Jenkins, our PO, would have said! The stains of the war years had been removed, and the mouldy looking green marble chips had been replaced with glistening new ones. The knee-high grass that had bordered the grave

now looked like a lawn, and there, in pride of place, was Bob's book! I had found it in old Turner's marble workshop. Splendid it now looked, carved in white marble. It was laid open and it read:

Flight Sgt. A. J. 'Bob' Kimberley RAF
Killed in action September 10, 1944
'Forever remembered'

The grave now gleamed as it had always done, amongst the

'I wonder what he would have thought of my demob suit.'

wilderness all around it. I stood there saying to myself, 'Well, old pal, remember Grandad saying, "All around the world". I nearly made it, but not quite, and look at me standing here with not a scratch to show for it.

'What did Bob say, up in North Wales three years ago? "The best is yet to come." Don't worry, Bob, I'll make it so for both of us!'

An hour later I walked down Clerkenwell Road. Nothing had

changed – bombed-out buildings still lined some of the pavements! I grabbed the brass handles that still shone as brightly as ever. I went up the staircase two at a time (old habits die hard), and stopped on the half landing to let two giggly girls go past. The cosy old warmth of the Counting House came flooding down the stairs to me. I smiled as I remembered them all up there. I was just 14 when I had first climbed these stairs as the office boy.

'Where's the "Cockney Kid"? they would bellow down the office. 'There's no sugar in my tea.'

Joe Cantor would say, 'Not enough cheese in my roll', and old Griff would complain, 'My inkwell wants filling!'

I was 17½ years old when I left for the Navy, and was the proud owner of my very own ledger, unheard of in pre-war days for somebody so young! Just one more step up the stairs and I knew I would become part of it all again.

But did I really want it – ledgers, statements, invoices, inkwells? No, I wanted something different. There must be other things for me to do.

I turned and went back down the stairs and left them all to it!

Love at first sight

When Sylvia left the comptometer office in the Counting House to join the ATS or something like, Yvonne took her place.

For me it was love at first sight when, later that same day, I was standing on the platform at Liverpool Street Station, it was raining hard and I was drenched because all the glass in the roof had long since gone, thanks to the Blitz. I couldn't believe my luck, for at the other end of the platform, there she was, waiting to get the same train home as me. My luck was really in that day, because, like me, she got off the train at Romford. In fact, we lived half an hour's walk from each other, and it wasn't long before we were sitting in the one-and-sixes in the 'Havana' cinema in Romford.

I wrote to Bob, who was in far-off Canada endeavouring to get his wings up, and told him of my good fortune, spelling out her name in full, Yvonne Maria Johnson Smith – how about that!

'Crikey' he replied, 'how did I miss a girl with a name like that when I was back in Hornchurch?' He went on to say that he was perfecting his flying skills, looping the loop over the Rockies, and that when he wasn't flying he was swotting like mad on all the technical things. 'No time for girls, kid,' he wrote.

I replied, 'Oh yeah, tell me another one!'

Bombed out of E13, the Balaam Street boys went their separate ways, but it wasn't too long before me, Alf, Ernie, Arthur, Eddy, Chas and other new-found mates joined forces again, meeting up in the local park for the time-honoured kick-about. Coats, as ever, were laid down for goal posts. It was just like the good old days. Well, it wasn't too many days ago!

From office boy, tending the ledger clerks' requirements in the Counting House, I was now one myself – the days were gone of ensuring that Joe Cantor had two lumps of sugar in his tea, Ben Tollhurst none at all, old Griff for ever telling me to take his cheese roll back to Madge, who owned the café across the way in St John's Square, demanding that more marge be spread on his roll, and Alice Pratt saying that her roll was too crusty for her liking.

Madge would storm at me, 'You go and tell them that there's a war on.' I never dared do that. So, by nicking a piece of cheese off this one, a bit of butter here, and swapping Alice's roll for Joe Cantor's, I was able to satisfy one and all. It was with relief that I handed my office boy's duties to some other poor unfortunate!

Of course, my luck with Yvonne had to run out. Dusk was falling when we called it a day for our weekly kick-about. Picking up our coats and getting on our bikes, I couldn't believe my eyes when up the path came Yvonne, arm in arm with some Air Force erk from the local RAF station. My heart went down into the bottom of my muddy football boots.

I caught up with her as she was crossing St John's Square on the way to the station. 'What happened last night?' I asked. 'What's wrong?'

'Oh, nothing,' she replied as cool as a cucumber. 'Just that I'm fed up with you and your silly football games,' she sniffed, 'just like a lot of schoolboys, kicking and chasing a ball about the park.' Then, with another sniff, 'Anyway, I prefer older men!' She was 16 and I a little older! She stalked off, leaving me alone with the pigeons in the Square.

For me, the Counting House became old, musty and humdrum. My ledger no longer had its appeal of a few months ago. The exhilaration I enjoyed through getting to work come bombs, rain or shine had long since gone. Till then, us Balaam Street boys weren't at all bothered that old Hitler's armies were just 50 miles away. On all fronts there was bad news. North Africa was like a seesaw, bigger and bigger losses were reported from the Atlantic, but we continued on our merry way.

We biked around the Essex countryside at the weekends, without a signpost to see us on our way (they had all been removed when the threat of invasion was at its height). Saturday evenings and maybe Sundays too were spent at the pictures. The war, we thought, was more for grown-ups!

The Counting House became drearier to me, and Yvonne kept her distance. 'I'll join up,' I thought. Not old enough yet, but I had read that the Merchant Navy took lads on at 16.

'That's it,' I thought, 'I'll join the Merchant Navy.' That's it, blow my old ledger, the Counting House, and blow, too, Yvonne Maria Johnson Smith!

Cough

'...and I was in the 'Andrew'.

The Merchant Navy's seamen's pool was in Leman Street, Aldgate, a 20-minute tram ride from Clerkenwell. 'Closed' said the notice on the door – 'Closed at 12 noon on Saturdays'.

'I'll try again next week,' I thought. I'll creep out of the office early on Saturday, asking Ben Tollhurst to cover for me, should the manager, Mr Stephens, ask of my whereabouts! But I still never made Leman Street in time! It never occurred to me to phone or write.

I told mum of my plans; she was upset and cross. 'Don't you think I've enough to worry about,' she said, 'what with Bob thousands of miles away wondering how he is every waking hour, old Silberstein up at Hackney urging me and the girls to turn out more and more battledress, and travelling in the blackout?' She leaned back in the fireside chair, looking worn out and weary. 'There's plenty of time for you to go off and do your bit,' she said with a smile, adding, 'You're not 20 yet.'

'Oh, all right, Mum, I didn't think it'd upset you. I'll forget the idea.' I did and never went back to Leman Street again!

The months hurried past. Bob was doing well in Canada. He got his cherished wings up, but was confined to Canada for another three months. 'Another b——

course,' he wrote. 'I'm fed up with them.'

'Mum,' I said. 'I'll have to volunteer soon, cos if not I'll end up in the Army and I don't want that!'

'You'll be going in the RAF like Bob, then?'

'Oh no, it's the Navy for me!'

Old Murray's Friday afternoon lectures down at Balaam Street School had put me off the Army for ever. His reminiscences of life in the trenches in the First World War, freezing mud, bayonets, barbed wire and what have you, gave me the creeps. He had seen it all and had first-hand knowledge, and was endeavouring to instil into his lads the horrors and futility of war!

'B—— old quack...'

Alas, old Hitler had put paid to his wishful thinking!

I walked along the corridor in the Drill Hall. 'Doctor Reid M.O.' read the small notice on the door.

'Come in,' the voice said. Bob had mentioned that when he went up for his medical he recognised old Dr Reid from our Plaistow days. 'Crikey,' he said at the time, 'they must have got him out of retirement for the duration,' and here he was still at it!

Of course, he didn't recognise me, or the name, but I remembered the time when he sent me off to some isolation hospital in far-away Kent, fearing that I had some fearful disease. 'B—— old quack,' Grandad called him when I arrived home the next day with a mild dose of chickenpox!

'Cough,' he asked of me. I obliged. 'You'll do,' he said, adding, 'Bit underweight, young man – no doubt the Navy's food will put a bit of meat on your bones.'

I thanked him and hurried down the corridor to the next door. 'CPO Williams' it said.

'Now lad, why did you volunteer and wish to join the Royal Navy?' he asked.

'Er, er, well, cos I like the sea.'

'And no doubt a girl in every port, eh?' he said with a twinkle in his eye. 'Pen-pusher are you?' as he took down my particulars. 'Right-

oh, you'll be hearing from us in seven to eight weeks time – just sign here,' indicating the place with his

finger. 'Mind you, if and when you're called up you decide the Navy's not for you, you can leave,' he added. 'That, of course, means the Army or the coal mines if you do change your mind – you'll have 14 days to think about it.' I hurried along South Street to the station to catch the train to Liverpool Street and tell them of my news, and Yvonne could put that in her pipe and smoke it!

Crikey, it's a Gerry!

We heard the rat-tat-tat of machine-gun fire.

Sitting on the train I had the compartment all to myself. I thought of that morning some years before when I was on the early morning workmen's train (you had to arrive in Liverpool Street sharp at 8am – if you didn't you had to pay the full fare, and the Workmen's was only a shilling return!). I had a corner seat like now, and flying low the lone fighter plane had skimmed the top of the gasworks, zooming towards us.

'Crikey, it's a Gerry!' I could clearly see the black and white crosses on its wings. 'Cor, look! There's a Spit on its tail!'

We had heard the rat-tat-tat of machine-gun fire as they zoomed over us. There had been no room to dive on the floor because the compartment, as on all workmen's trains, was packed. There was no time, anyway – as quickly as they had come, they had roared away, and the 7.30am train from Romford, unconcerned, had chugged on its way to Liverpool Street.

Today I climbed the stone steps and reached for the brass handle, as I had done for the first time three years earlier when I had just left school. I knocked at Mr Rodgers's office door.

'Come in,' he called.

Looking up at the tall windows in his office thinking, 'He'll have to get somebody else to put up the blackout blinds!', I told him my news.

'Sorry to lose you, Kimberley,' he said, adding, 'You'll want the customary seven days off before you go, I expect?'

'Yes please, sir,' I replied.

As I went along to my desk and opened the old ledger I looked across at them all perched up on their high stools. Ben Tollhurst, old Griff the senior clerk, Alice Pratt and Griffen – I would miss them all. Three years ago they had called me the 'Cockney Kid', and I still was at heart and proud of it. In their good time and way, slowly and unbeknown to me, they had knocked off the rough edges!

When I took over my own ledger at 16, unheard of in earlier days, they couldn't have been more kind and helpful. But now it was time for me to close the old ledger, and get on with other things.

I would miss them all.

HMS Glendower

'There you are, boys' the Wren said, pointing out of the window, 'there's your home for the next three months. That's HMS *Glendower*, the ship that will never go to sea!'

We looked out with her, anxious now to see what lay in store for us.

'Yes,' she said, 'that's Billy Butlin's former holiday camp in North Wales!'

The rows of chalets disappeared from view as the local train came to a halt at Pwllheli Station. It was a late August evening. The day had started early in the Drill Hall at Romford, then we had moved on to the station – Liverpool Street to Euston, on to Crewe, Crewe to Chester, Chester to Bangor. And now here, at long last, Pwllheli.

As I lifted my case from the rack that funny feeling came into my tummy, as it did when old Emmet ushered us into the swimming baths down at Balaam Street; I even imagined the carbolicky smell coming up under my nostrils. We trooped along the platform and got into the waiting coach. Twenty minutes later we climbed off.

'Good luck boys, have a nice holiday!' the Wren called out.

'Get in line along here,' the peaked cap called out. We did as he asked. 'I am going to call your names out, just answer "Here" when I call yours, understood?'

The officer came from the guard house. 'All present and correct, Chief?' he asked.

'Aye aye, sir.'

'That will be the lot for the day, Chief. Wheel them away, will you?'

As we stumbled away with the Chief, a bugle sounded. I could see the ensign come fluttering down from a distant yard-arm. We passed through rows of chalets and were subjected to all sorts of taunts.

'Go back home while you have the chance … you're better off in the Army … the square bashing will murder you!'

'Take no notice, lads,' the Chief said. 'They've only been here a week themselves!'

He ushered the weary, worn-out group of would-be matelots into a large hall. There we joined a hundred or so more would-be matelots, who were standing in front of a large stage.

He came on the stage, with four rings on his sleeve, and either side of him stood the other Officers. He held up his hand. The general hubbub died away, and his gold braid glittered in the stage light.

'Welcome to HMS *Glendower*. I am Captain Barker, with me is my Commander and First Lieutenant. The *Glendower* will never sail away, but believe me – myself, and all my fellow Officers, Chief and Petty Officers will leave no stone unturned to give you the basic RN training that life at sea will demand of you. We have experience in peacetime and in war to make sailors of you. If we find that in the coming weeks you are not for us, we will tell you so. Likewise, if you don't like us here at *Glendower* in the next 14 days, you are free to leave. Is that clear?

'The training will be long, hard and vigorous, but I am sure you will find it enjoyable!' With a smile he added, 'To a point! In the next few days you will be appointed to a class, with your own Petty Officer in charge. You will also have a Divisional Officer. Any problems you may have that arise when you are at *Glendower* – service matters or domestic ones – request to see him.' Then, with another smile, 'Be assured that you'll find him human! Finally to you all, good luck and God bless you.'

He turned to his First Lieutenant saying, 'Get these men to their supper. They've had a long day and must be starving!'

'*…that funny feeling came into my tummy…*'

Kitting out

Bang, bang, bang, he bashed on the chalet door. 'Heavo, heavo, lash up and stow!' he bawled as he went down the line of chalets.

'Oh b—— off!' someone muttered. We all felt the same way, but quickly changed our tune when we heard the same din coming back up the line of chalets. The door burst open as, leaping from our bunks, our feet touched the floor.

'Well, well, what a b—— shambles!' said PO Taff Jenkins, finding us with one leg in our trousers, one sock on, one sock off.

'Where's my shirt?' someone wailed.

'Ten minutes!' he bawled, 'And I want to see you washed, dressed and lined up outside. The 'eads are at the end of the row of chalets!' And with that he was off.

'What's the 'eads?' somebody asked.

'You're colour blind.'

'It's where you get a wash and a pee!' somebody else volunteered.

Then Taff marched us off to the dining hall. 'Half hour you've got,' he said, adding, 'We've a lot to do today!' He counted off on his fingers. 'No 1 medical, No 2 eye test, No 3 pay books and station cards, that's if the MO thinks you're fit enough for us, No 4 injections – that'll sort out the men from the boys, that's for sure! Then, all being well, getting kitted out. Got it?'

The medical was a piece of cake, though much more thorough than old Dr Reid had given me in the Drill Hall some months ago. Oh, but the eye test was a disaster for me! 'You're colour blind,' the Wren Officer said as I sat opposite her, not being able to distinguish anything at all from the multi-coloured array of dots and spots that were in the book that lay open in front of me! She guided me into a darkened passage, where two tiny spots of light seemed miles away. 'Which one is green, and which on is red?' she asked.

I could see the spots, but, 'Red or Green? They both look the same to me!'

'You're colour blind,' she repeated, adding, 'We'll never make a sailor of you.'

In a panic I thought 'Will they send me home? Is it to be the Army after all?' And seeing Yvonne with an RAF bloke had put me off that mob, excepting old Bob of course!

'Well now, what are we going to do with you? How about the writing branch of the Navy?'

'The writing branch, Miss?'

'Ma'am,' she corrected me.

'Sorry, Miss, I mean Ma'am. I've had enough of writing!' I added, explaining that since leaving school I had done nothing else down at Clerkenwell.

'Oh,' she said. 'How is Holborn looking these days, and Gamages? I was a buyer there before the war.'

We returned to what she was going to do with me. Looking through my papers, she said, 'Seems you're a bright young man. Ah, here we are – this job will suit you down to the ground.'

'What's that, Ma'am?' I asked.

'RDF, or Radar as our American friends call it! But call it what you like, it helped us to win the Battle of Britain. Without it you or I wouldn't be sitting here today. It's helping us win the Battle of the Atlantic, and eventually it'll help us win the war! It's our secret eyes, enabling us to see Gerry before he can see us! It'll be right up your street. I'll put your name forward for a course, once you've finished the square-bashing here at *Glendower*, all right?'

'Oh, thanks, Ma'am,' I said, relieved now that the Army or the Air Force wouldn't be getting their hands on me! I thanked her again.

She smiled and said, 'Good luck, sailor.'

I was relieved that I didn't pass out.

Injections were another piece of cake, though for some it wasn't so. I was relieved that I didn't pass out like some unfortunates. Pay cards and station cards were acquired and filled in, and we were off to be kitted out. It was nearly dark as we filed into the long shed. We moved slowly along the counter, taking from the Wrens different items of clothing as we shuffled along. It was all done by guesswork on their part as each Wren eyed us up and down.

'No 4 size will do you,' said one, whatever No 4 size was.

'No 9s will do you fine.' Another Wren handed me a pair of boots.

When I reached the end of the long counter I had collected two jumpers, two pairs of bell-bottoms to be known as No 1s and No 3s, two collars, two shirt fronts, one black ribbon, two pairs of pants, two vests, two pairs of socks, one pair of boots, one cap, one cap band, one oilskin, one overcoat, one pair of overalls, one housewife (pocket sewing outfit), one lanyard and one seaman's manual.

'That'll do for you, jack,' the cheerful little Wren said. 'Move along the counter, find an empty spot and get your name and number marked on everything.' I found an empty spot and stamped everything with my name and number: CJX 557323.

'You're supposed to carry 'em, not drop 'em,' an impatient PO Taff Jenkins said to some unfortunate as he dropped his heap of clothing at the PO's feet. We slowly assembled outside. 'Right, off to your suppers now,' he said, adding, 'if there's any left. I want to see you all in the rig of the day – that's No 3s – outside at 08.30 hours in the morning. I've appointed O/S Davis as your class leader. The class is No 258. Class leader, see that the class is mustered on time!' He finished with, 'Got it?'

We hurried off to our chalets, dumped our kit, chased across to the mess hall and gobbled down our suppers!

The first parade

We were in some sort of line when he eyed us up and down. 'Well, well, well, what 'ave we got 'ere then?' He walked slowly past, fixing this and straightening that on our uniforms, which just about fitted in places! 'Get those backs straight, keep those backsides tucked in, and for sure it's you lot for the barber's shop tomorrow! Class leader fall out and get the tallest men to one end of the class and so on to the shortest, got it?'

'OK, PO,' the class leader replied.

Taff Jenkins exploded. 'OK? OK? It's "Aye aye, PO" and don't you lot ever forget it.'

We all waited for his 'Got it?'

After lots of sorting out with our sizes, I found myself up front. 'On the order of left turn, turn left. Left turn!' he bawled. We did as he asked more by luck than judgement! 'Right now, we're off to the parade ground to see what you're really made of. Quick march!'

He told us in no uncertain terms that we were the clumsiest lot of recruits he had come across, adding, 'But believe me, when you leave *Glendower*, class No 258 is going to be the best class ever! I warn you, though, don't make it too hard a job for me!'

'Stand easy,' was piped across the parade ground and we thankfully lit up our fags!

We improved slowly and surely as the weeks passed. I was getting confident now as, being one of the tallest; I led Class No 258 with another lofty, Harry Beamish from Sydenham! Right wheel, left turn,

about turn, quick march – of course we made the usual mess-ups, losing concentration when thinking of home. Believe me, our Taff Jenkins didn't allow that to happen too often!

We got shore leave and caught the 'liberty boat', a clapped-out old chara, that once a week on Saturdays took us into Pwllheli. We went to the flicks, which reminded me of the old Greengate cinema at Plaistow. The weeks hurried past and Taff Jenkins found it harder and harder to catch us out on the parade ground. His brisk orders were carried out to a T, the class moving as one; in fact, I was enjoying myself, being up front with my new mate Harry!

Every so often the coach turned up bringing new recruits and we gave them the reception that we had endured some weeks before!

I wrote home as often as I could; there wasn't much to write home about, except to say, 'I'm all right, hope you're all right, love Ken.' In Mum's letters back to me there was more often than not a 10 shilling note.

Each night I climbed up into my bunk. 'The Andrew's not too bad after all!' I thought. I pulled the hairy old blanket over me, wondering how they all were in the Counting House down at Clerkenwell and, of course, Yvonne. 'Oh, blow her!' I thought as I turned over and fell asleep.

It reminded me of the Greengate pictures down at Plaistow.

Old pals together again

A week later, during a stand-easy, 'Ordinary Seaman K. Kimberley report to the Post Office' was piped over the tannoy. It ended with, 'At the double!'

We all looked at each other. 'Crikey!' they said, pointing at me. 'That's you!'

I chased to the Post Office and, all out of breath, said to the duty Wren, 'I'm O/S Kimberley.'

'Oh yes, there's a telegram for you.' My heart was missing beats as I read it.

'Good news is it, I hope?' she asked as she saw the look of relief flood over me.

'Oh yes,' I answered. 'It's my brother Bob – he's home from Canada and is coming up here to see me on Saturday!'

Square-bashing was over for the week and with the others I got into my No 1s, making sure that the white front was spotless and that the collar and the bow on my black ribbon were right. I gave my boots an extra shine. It was a fine autumn day as we climbed aboard the old chara that rumbled its way down the lanes into Pwllheli. It dropped us off in the square opposite the Pwllheli Arms Hotel where Bob would be staying for the weekend. I spotted him standing on the steps,

and he waved when he saw me amongst the others. 'Hello kid!' he called out.

''ullo Bobby!' I called back.

'How about that drink we've been promising ourselves?' he said as he led the way into the bar. 'What's it going to be?'

'Oh, I'll have a black and tan.'

'What's that?'

'Er, it's a half of bitter and a half of Guinness,' I replied.

'Crikey! You've grown up fast!'

'Well, all the lads drink it.'

'And you don't want to be the odd man out, eh?'

'Well, you know how it is.'

''Course I do, kid, 'course I do!'

'Chris'll will be down in a minute.'

'Chris?' I asked.

'You remember Chris, surely.' Along with a few others back home, I remembered Chris as a bit of a blonde bombshell! Her uncle owned the Chequers pub, our local, and on occasions Chris helped out behind the bar. She soon became a regular around the Sunday tea table – along with a few others, I might add. 'We've got ourselves engaged – she's the one for me Ken. I realised this when I was in Canada! There's nobody else now! She thinks the same way, so from now on kid, it's

the straight and narrow for me!' He broke off as Chris came into the bar.

Over dinner we chatted like two schoolboys. Chris was content to sit back and let us get on with it!

'What are you going to get up to in the RN?' he asked. I told him of my colour blindness stopping me from becoming a proper seaman and of my forthcoming radar course. 'Oh,' he said. 'They can stick all the seamanship stuff, Ken – get stuck into this radar course. I know a bit about it. These new ideas, Ken, it's like planes –they'll be a thing of the future!'

Back in the bar I asked him about Canada. 'Smashing country, Ken, you'd like it. I managed a few days in New York on my way back to the UK. Gosh, Ken, what a place that is!' He leaned back in the big armchair, 'But there's no place like home kid. Home sweet home, there's no place like it!'

The waiter came in and drew the curtains.

'Crikey!' I said. 'What's the time, cos the liberty boat leaves the square at 21.30 hours!' Bob turned to Chris, saying with a laugh, '21.30 hours – what's that all about? Liberty boat – what's that?'

Ten minutes later we stood on the steps. 'Look after yourself,' I said to him.

'Oh, I'll be all right – nothing's going to happen to me. It's you

we're all worried about.' He took some pound notes and stuffed them inside my jumper. 'I know you could do with these. I'm paying you back for all those tube fares you gave me when I used to bunk home from Regents Park, remember? Don't forget, when this b—— nuisance of a war is over we'll make up for all this lost time!'

He turned to Chris. 'Won't we, Chris?'

I hurried over to the waiting chara, turned and waved to them as they stood on the hotel steps. Later, back in the chalet, I took off my jumper and as I did ten £1 notes fell to the floor.

'Cor!' they all said. 'Wish I had a brother in the RAF!'

Sunday divisions

We lined up for Sunday morning 'divisions', standing easy with gaiters on. PO Jenkins nodded his approval. We could see the Captain making his way slowly down the line of Class No 257, the Commander and the First Lieutenant in tow. Old PO Thomas, who wet-nursed Class 257, followed at a respectable distance. As the party came to the end of Class 257 Taff Jenkins barked, 'Slope arms!' By now we could carry out this command in our sleep. As I slung the rifle up to my shoulder and came to attention, I spotted, in the far distance, the local train from Pwllheli to Bangor. Bob and Chris were on the first leg of their journey back home. I thought of Bob's words, 'Home sweet home', and got that horrible 'Balaam Street Baths' feeling in my tummy and, of course, with it that carbolicky smell.

'Pick it up, pick if up, you long streak of p——,' I heard PO Jenkins call out. I looked down in horror at my rifle, which had slipped out of my grasp and now lay on the parade ground. I heard the sniggers around me and hoped the earth would swallow me up! I bent down and picked it up, noticing the Captain leave Class 257 and make his way, thankfully, to the other end of our class. One last glare from Taff Jenkins and he went off to escort the Captain down the line. For a while I was no longer known as 'lofty' but 'butter fingers', and was our PO's public enemy No 1!

The days passed quickly enough; we eased up on the square-bashing and began learning about other aspects of life at sea.

'Gather round,' said Taff, handing us each a length of thin rope. 'The next few days we're going to eat, sleep and dream about knots.' He added, 'You'll find them all in your "Bible". You're to read all about them so that you can do them blindfolded. Got it?'

Sheet bends, double sheet bends, reef knots, he had us doing them all, and we often tied ourselves up in knots in the process!

'Now, this is the bowline on the bight. One day it could save your life If you go overboard and somebody throws you a line, this is the knot you secure the line with. That's if you're alive to do it, of course! It'll never let you down, cos the tighter the line is pulled the more secure the knot becomes!' We waited for the 'Got it?' 'If you can't tie a bowline, you might as well pack your bags now and join the b—— Army!'

'If you can't tie a bowline...'

Boat drill

It was a fine morning when he marched us off to the Bay. 'Boat drill,' he said. 'This'll bring on the aches and pains for you!'

We pushed the whaler out. 'Clinker-built she is,' he said. 'You can tell clinker by the way each plank overlaps. Carver-built is when the planks butt to each other.' He went up to the tiller – I think that's what he called it.

'Right, make yourselves comfortable.' We sat there, waiting for the next order, the whaler gently rocking on the surf. 'Pick up an oar each!' This was easier said than done – eight feet long they seemed. 'In the rowlocks with 'em.' Again, this was no easy task, but eventually each oar found its rightful home.

'Right! When I give the order "Oars", lift the oar out of the rowlock to an upright position!'

In doing this we almost capsized the whaler. A dozen or so oars tottered and weaved about like bean poles in a gale! The knack, we soon learned, was to use your knees as a sort of lever to get the oars into a steady upright position. Then we lowered them back into their rightful position with a big sigh of relief.

'Pull together!' he roared, and again more by luck than judgement we managed it! Square-bashing is a bit of cake compared to this skylark, I thought, as I watched the blade of the oar dip in and out, in and out of the waves! A peaceful row on the lake in Barking Park with my old mates seemed a world away!

A roar like an express train – two, maybe three express trains – put Barking Park right out of my head as eight or so low-flying aircraft skimmed the waves and zoomed over us! They were gone as quickly as they had come, but not before Taff Jenkins let them know what he thought of them. 'B—— Brylcreem Boys, I'll 'ave your guts for garters!' He voiced a few other choice remarks as the Beaufighters roared away and disappeared over the Welsh hills.

We managed to steady the rocking whaler and got her back to the pebbly beach while Taff went on about those so and so's!

I remembered Bob saying, when we met up, that he was attached to an operational training squadron flying 'Beaus' near Carlisle, and he hinted that the squadron used the Welsh terrain as ideal training ground for low-level attacks. In the chalet that evening I didn't dare tell them that it was probably Bob who nearly gave us all a ducking.

Meanwhile we all compared our blistered hands…

'Oars!'

Gun drill

My mate, all excited like, came into the chalet one evening after we had secured for the day.

'I've been talking to one of the girls in the NAAFI,' he said, 'and she mentioned that we've a tailor on board. He's a Petty Officer, she said. Don't know his name, but you'll find him in the POs' quarters.'

That was good news for us because we were fed up with our ill-fitting No 1s. The trousers were like drain-pipes, not a bit like bell-bottoms, and the jumpers fitted like sacks for most of us.

Later we stumbled around the POs' chalets in the dark. 'Knock 'ere and ask where the tailor lives.' They pushed me forward to do the knocking and the asking.

'Come in,' a voice answered. That sounds familiar, I thought. I looked around the half-opened door and got the surprise of a lifetime. There beneath a naked electric light bulb sat our own Taff Jenkins. I recognised the sewing machine because it was just like the one back home that Mum used. He looked up.

'What do you want?' he asked.

'Er, are you the tailor?'

'Well, er, PO, are you the tailor?' I asked.

'Well, I ain't scotch mist, that's for sure!'

'Er, will you do some alterations for us?' I asked. He reached for a well-worn board and gave it to me. It read, '2 inch gussets in trousers – 2/6d; let-ins or let-outs – 2/-'.

'Take seven days, if you bring 'em tomorrow.' I waited for the customary 'Got it!' It never came. Instead, 'Tell your lot there's gun drill first thing tomorrow. We'll be there all day and overalls is rig of the day – got it?'

I closed the door, re-arranging the blackout curtain as I did so. I told the blokes who the tailor was.

'Crikey!' they exclaimed. 'I bet he's worth a few bob, cos he's been here since the war started. He must have altered a lot of No 1s since then!'

The following day Taff Jenkins marched us to a long low wood shed. It all looked mysterious. There were no windows and it was on the very edge of the camp.

'Halt!' he barked. Then, with his customary 'Right!', he continued. 'I want the first ten in the shed, the rest of you to stand easy outside. No smoking, do you hear?' I was one of the ten. 'Off with your boots and put these wellingtons on.'

He handed us each in turn anti-flash hoods and gloves. In the dim light we could make out, on a platform, what seemed to be a gun. It looked just like the real thing. Rows of shells and cordite cases lined the walls around it.

He lined us up. 'You're the loader,' he said to me, explaining what my responsibilities were, then those of the others. 'Got it? You know what you all have to do then? Right, we'll have a dummy run, shall we? When I blow my whistle, run through the drill as I've described. You'll hear the order over the tannoy: "Commence, commence, commence". That's when you get going.'

We did a few dummy runs in the dismal light and somehow with him bawling and yelling at us we muddled through. He must have been reasonably satisfied as he said, 'Now we'll try it in the conditions you may experience at sea!'

The dim light went out, and it was pitch black. Then an eerie yellow light came on, which outlined the gun platform. Mist and smoke whirled around us as it started to rain.

'Commence, commence,' we heard, and we dashed about in the near darkness, bashing into each other as we did so. After half a dozen runs, out of the chaos came some sort of order. We began to enjoy ourselves – it was like skylarking about in the playground back at school down Balaam Street. There were crashes and bangs; the noisier it became the more we

enjoyed it! Then too late, in the smoke and rain, I saw a wellington creep out and trip me up. Down I went, hanging on to the cordite case for dear life. As I hit the deck I felt the case bite deep into my finger, through the glove on my right hand.

He stood over me saying, 'It's you again, my public enemy No 1. You shouldn't be wearing fancy rings! Get him over to the sick bay!'

They cut Dad's ring in half to get it out of my knuckle, then bandaged my finger and put my arm in a sling. Then they gave me the two halves of Dad's ring that he had worn throughout the Great War! I went back to the shed and waited for the lads to come out.

'You back are you?' said Taff Jenkins when he spied me.

He surprised me when he asked, 'Are you all right lad? How's the ring?'

I showed him the two pieces.

'Never mind, son,' he said. 'A jeweller will be able to put that together again.' Our Taff was a bit of a softy at heart, I thought.

I handed him the sick bay chit showing him that I was excused all duties for two to three days. 'That's all right, Lofty. It'll give you time to get stuck into that seaman's manual of yours!'

The Isle of Sark

'It's not much bigger than the Woolwich Free Ferry.'

When we left the *Glendower* we felt that we were old sweats and swaggered about in our now wide bell-bottoms and tight-fitting jumpers, thanks to old Taff. We all went our separate ways to RNBs at Chatham, Pompey and Devonport, or some, like me, to different courses. The evening before, Taff Jenkins came to each chalet to wish us luck. 'Don't forget that "bowline on the bight"!' he reminded each one of us. We thanked him for his patience with us.

I wrote home, telling them of my new address: HMS *Isle of Sark*, c/o GPO London.

'I am off to sea,' I wrote. 'Don't worry, Mum, I'll only be going up and down the Clyde in Scotland learning all about radar.' 'What's that?' I could hear her saying. 'If I pass the course I should get seven days leave – how about that then? Look after yourself. Love, Ken xxxxx'

Two of us left *Glendower* for the radar course on the River Clyde. We reported to the RTO at Glasgow Central where 20 or more other matelots were waiting. With our kit bags and hammocks, we all scrambled on to an RN lorry, which took us through the blacked-out streets of Glasgow. An hour later we scrambled off again in a rain-swept dockyard in Greenock. A Leading Hand off the *Isle of Sark* guided us through and around all the usual dockyard paraphernalia,

over railway lines, discarded oil drums, anchor chains and anchors and so many other rusting hazards. A sentry stood at the bottom of the gangway. In the dim pilot light at the top, the reception party waited for us.

'Say "Present" when you hear your name called,' one of them said.

'Crikey!' Eddy muttered to me. 'It don't look much bigger than the Woolwich Free Ferry. I feel seasick already!'

We went below, were given a locker each and a place over the long mess tables to sling our hammocks. The next morning the Petty Officer introduced himself, then introduced us to the elementary principles of radar. After a week of theory, we each found ourselves, one at a time, locked up in a tiny cabin in front of a PPI (Plan Position Indicator). We had learned, off by heart now, how to switch everything on and off, a daunting task at the very beginning. We also learned how to speak to the bridge with the correct procedure.

When it was my turn in the cabin I donned the earphones and sat perched in front of the PPI. It was all switched on and the aerial was in automatic. In the gloom of the tiny cabin, I watched the scan. A thin green line swept around a full 360°. We were now out in the Firth of Clyde and there were lots of ships around us. That meant lots of

'echoes', as the thin line picked up each one with a bright green 'blip'. On the perimeter of the scan was the compass bearing going through 90o. Just above me was the range indicator, which, when you fixed the aerial on a chosen 'blip' gave the distance in yards.

I was nervous, as it was my first go. 'Bridge – radar,' snapped the Officer of the Watch in my ears. 'Give me the range and bearing of the ship dead ahead.'

'Aye aye, sir!'

With trembling fingers I flicked the automatic switch to manual. I found the ship that was dead ahead and with relief passed the bearing and range to the bridge every two minutes as he had asked. Requests for range and bearings came into my earphones thick and fast, but I coped. At last my watch came to an end. The cabin door opened and the PO said, 'Well done, lad, that's enough for today. Let somebody else 'ave a go!'

I was more than willing to comply, so informed the bridge that my watch was over and that I was handing over to O/S Benson.

'Carry on, O/S Kimberley,' snapped the Officer of the Watch.

And that's how it went on for four weeks. We quickly adapted to the *Isle of Sark*'s routine, tying up alongside at Greenock just as darkness fell. At long last we mastered the art of getting in and falling out of our hammocks. We

had the usual gripes and moans about that miserable old so and so on the bridge. We got to know when he was up there and did our

best to avoid him! Laying in our hammocks we listened to Vera Lynn and her 'White Cliffs of Dover' and 'We'll meet again.'

Then came the day when we assembled for the big test. We just hoped that old so and so wasn't up there on the bridge when it came

round to our turn for the final judgement. Unfortunately I copped him, but I must have done all right because at the end of 20 minutes he

said, 'Well done, O/S Kimberley!' and the PO said, 'You can get your needle and cotton out now and sew on that Radar badge.'

RNB Chatham

'I haven't been here a day yet.'

At Euston Station I struggled into the RTO with my hammock, kitbag and small suitcase. 'Is it London Bridge or Victoria for RNB Chatham?' I asked, not relishing the thought of trailing my worldly possessions across London.

'You're in luck, jack,' the Army bloke said. 'There's an RN lorry due here at any moment. He'll be going to London Bridge Station in about an hour. Time for a cuppa in the NAAFI,' he added. I was lucky again when I and some other matelots climbed up on to a waiting Navy lorry outside the station at Chatham. 'Nelson Block Mess No 3,' he said as he handed me my Station Card, a red one for port watch.

It was mid-afternoon when I heaved my hammock, kit bag and case up the stone staircase in the grim and cheerless Nelson Block. Mum had told me that her elder brother, my uncle Charlie Thompson, had served in the RN in the First World War and had been stationed at Chatham. Who knows, I thought, perhaps he had climbed these very stairs and pushed his way through the heavy worn old doors, as I was doing now. The floorboards ran right up to the open fireplace where a cheerful fire was blazing away. A Leading Seaman, with three badges up, was

sitting beside it. Mess tables, scrubbed white, lined the walls, and hammocks, lashed up, hung over them. Electric light bulbs under green shades hung low from the high ceiling, spreading patches of light here and there. Small paned windows were set high up in the walls just beneath the ceiling. It hasn't changed much since my Uncle Charlie's day, I thought.

I dragged my hammock and kit bag to the nearest bench and collapsed down on it.

'Stripey,' I called. 'Where can I sling my hammock?'

He didn't look up. 'Where there's an empty set of 'ooks,' he said.

Later I was surprised when 'ookey, the three-badge man, put an enamel cup of tea on the table in front of me.

'Do with this, son, I expect!'

'Cor, thanks, Stripey.'

'Just come in?' he asked.

'That's right,' I said, thinking that he should have been pensioned off before the war, his grey hairs giving the game away. But like many of his kind, he was in the Barracks for the duration. Chatham, Pompey, Devonport – they all had their share of Barrack Room Stanchions, as they were known! It was down to them that the mess looked so spotless and tidy. Nobody questioned their authority in the mess; they were a

law unto themselves, and knew every RN regulation!

'Got to do the "joining barracks routine" now, 'ave you?' he asked. 'Take my tip, lad, and take your time cos once that lot over there in the drill shed get to know you're 'ere, they'll 'ave you out again!' With that he went back to his stool by the cheerful fireplace and picked up his *Daily Mirror*. 'Bet he's a "Jane" fan,' I thought…

The next morning I stepped out on to the pavement and admired the immaculate beds of wallflowers and daffodils that were just peeping through the well-laid-out bed in front of the ornate stone balustrade that ran the length of the parade ground below. 'Gosh,' I thought, 'you wouldn't think there was a war on!' Through the greyness of it all, it gleamed and sparkled. I went down the stone steps. Everywhere there were working parties armed with brooms and shovels. A PO was putting a line of defaulters through their paces! Stripey had told me that the offices where I had to sign on were at the far side of the drill shed.

'Don't forget, lad, take your time!' He meant well, I thought, but I was due seven days leave and the sooner I got through this 'joining barracks' lark, I could put in for it! I jumped out of my skin when the tannoy barked out in all four corners of the parade ground.

'Ordinary Seaman Radar K. Kimberley CJX 557323 report to the Foreign Service Draft Office.' There was a pause. 'Now!' it finished.

'Can't be me, can't be me – I 'aven't been in a day yet. Must be another me in here,' I thought.

'Foreign Service Draft Office' the board read. 'Knock and Wait' the notice said. The window slid open.

'I'm O/S Kimberley – you piped for me,' I said, adding, 'There's a mistake – I 'aven't been here a day yet!'

The face said, 'There's no mistake, sonny Jim. You Radar boys are popular with us! You're the one we want. Go along to the Leave Office, Pay Office and Victualling Office – they'll give you all the necessary!'

'But – but you're sure it's me you want?'

He ignored the question. 'Look,' he said. 'Just make sure you report back here in 14 days time at 0900 hours.' With that the window slammed shut with a bang!

I looked around me at all the hustle and bustle. Foreign Service, 14 days leave? I brightened up, thinking of 14 long days at home! I called in at the various offices, hurried back across the parade ground, and bounded up the more cheerful-looking stairs to Mess No 3.

'Yippee!' I thought. 'I'll be home for Christmas!'

The Andes

'The war will be over before we get there.'

I woke up for the umpteenth time since leaving the dockyard at Chatham as the train stopped. So too did Jack, whom I had palled up with in my brief stay at Chatham.

'Where are we?' he grumbled.

I lifted the blackout blind a few inches and rubbed the condensation away with my fingers.

'It's a station.' I was aware of RAF lads moving along the platform, spotting the tiny white flashes in their caps, just like Bob wore in his early days. 'Gosh!' I thought, 'They're air crew trainees.' The mystery for me was solved. 'We're either going to Canada or the States, cos that's where Bob did his flying training!'

Earlier, as we had piled our kit bags and the rest into the luggage vans at Chatham, we had read the label stuck on the door: 'Draft No 315,' it read. 'Ex Chatham for Liverpool Dockside/*Andes*.' Seeing those white flashes had solved the mystery of our destination, and with a jolt and a jerk we were off again.

I stood up, looking at the dismal light wreathed in fag smoke as it curled its lazy way around the carriage ceiling. I stepped over outstretched legs and feet and went out into the corridor – at least the air was fresher out here! I leaned on the brass rail that stretched across the window and looked out into the darkness. I thought of a week ago when I had been back home. Gee,

Mum had done wonders to make Christmas as it had always been. Despite food rationing she had performed miracles – still, that was Mum! The fly in the ointment was that Bob hadn't been at home to share it all. I had sent him a telegram on the first day of my leave, asking him if he could get a few days off. Early the next day, Lily Green from the corner shop had knocked and told Mum that Bob was on the phone, and could he speak to Ken? I hurried back to the shop with her.

'Can't make it, kid – believe me, I've tried my hardest to get a few days, but they won't hear of it.'

'Don't worry, Bob, they'll be plenty of other Christmases.'

'You bet,' he said. We talked for a few more moments. 'I'll write to you, right now,' he said.

His letter turned up a few days before Christmas Day. It worried me a bit; he sounded fed up and depressed. 'I'm fed up with this b—— outfit at times like this,' he wrote. 'I'm certain we have nothing on for a week or so, but the silly old s—— of a CO lectured me, saying that many brothers had to spend Christmas apart. That's not the point, is it? Because he could have easily given me 48 hours. I feel like b——ing off, but as you know they'll be hot on passes at this time of the year!' The letter went on: 'Look after yourself, Ken – we'll all be back together again one of these

fine days when this b—— lousy war is over!'

The day my leave was over Mum had a letter from him saying that Chris and he had decided to get married on his next leave!

I went back to my corner seat and dozed off. Next thing I knew the Transport PO called out, 'Wakey, wakey, lads! All change!' He slid open the compartment door. 'Come on out of it and let's 'ave you out on the platform, else the war will be over before we get there!'

We went up to the luggage van. Two lads got up into it and threw our worldly possessions out on to the platform, calling out the names on the labels as they did so. The smell of salt and oily water was strong. The *Andes* towered above us. It was still dark and the cold night air, after the stuffiness of the compartment, took my breath away.

'Get fell in lads!' the PO called out, and with that he led us up the ship's gangway.

'What would old Grandad think about this then,' I wondered, thinking of those early days when he took Bob and me down to the docks to see the big ships off. 'Where are they going, Grandad?' we used to ask. I saw us sitting round the kitchen table with our atlas open, and now here I was acting out those distant memories for real!

Lifeboat drill

We got sorted out on a mess deck and slung our hammocks; we were so short of space that they touched each other. Nevertheless, it was a relief to get sorted out and settled down.

'This is the Captain speaking!' came the voice from the tannoy. 'Welcome aboard the *Andes*. We will be casting off in approximately one hour's time. I can now tell you that our destination is New York. Our ETA will be 0800 hours, 10.1.44. Weather and Gerry, of course, permitting! The majority of RN personnel on board, on arrival in New York, will proceed to Asbury Park, New Jersey. The remainder to Boston, Massachusetts. The RAF people will proceed to Texas or California. Be assured that our US friends will welcome you and be most generous to you.' There were loud cheers when he said this! 'I must warn you that the weather for the next two to three days won't be to your liking, but for the remainder of the trip it should be fair! I ask you all to be patient in the queues at mealtimes. As you will appreciate we have many mouths to feed!' Groans at this! 'At all times adhere to the ship's rules and regulations and be sure to know where your life-jackets are at all times. That is all!'

A three-badge Leading Seaman came into our mess and introduced himself. 'I'm Leading Seaman Sarkey. I'm here to wet nurse you till we get to the other side. You know from your boarding cards what lifeboat station number you are. So let's not waste any time and go up and find it! And don't – *don't* – forget your lifebelts!'

He knew the *Andes* like the back of his hand, having done this trip many times before! Before the war she had been a cruise liner in the Caribbean, and moving along passageways and up stairways we eventually found ourselves on the Boat Deck at Station No 3.

'Right,' he said. 'This is where we muster if there's any trouble. Do as I say at all times and we'll get along fine!'

The Liver Building, birds and all, and the Liverpool dockside were slowly slipping behind us as the *Andes* got under way.

Leading Seaman Sarkey dismissed us, saying, 'Take my advice and get down to the dining hall for the midday meal.'

'But it's only 10.00 hours, 'ookey!' somebody piped up.

'Look! Just do as I say and less of the back-chat!' he said, with a firmness in his voice. There was no more back-chat.

We did as he advised us and three hours later we were at the head of the queue into the dining hall.

Dinner time

On arriving at the top of the grand staircase that led down into the vast dining hall, we looked about us in bewilderment, having never seen the likes of it before, except at the pictures!

Although the walls were partly boarded up, the exotic paintings stretched up to the ceiling. Birds of paradise and giant butterflies weaved their way through the painted foliage. Giant flower-like chandeliers vied for space on the ceiling supported by gold-tipped palm trees rising up from the floor. 'Cor,' somebody said, 'it's just like 'ollywood. Where's Carmen Miranda?'

We came down to earth with a bump when we viewed the scene below us. Stark metal canteen tables and benches and the familiar tea urn at the head of each table reminded us that we were still in the 'Andrew'. The chatter from so many hundreds of Navy and RAF blokes, the clatter of tin trays –

crikey, it was just like *Glendower* and *Chatham* rolled into one! It was worth all the queuing, though, because the food, we all agreed, was the best we had had since being in the 'Andrew'. We filled our trays to overflowing and gobbled it down as quickly as we could, as if it was to be our last meal on land or sea!

The morning after the night before

'You'll be better for some fresh air inside you.'

Our wet nurse weaved and ducked his way around the heaving and swaying hammocks.

'Wakey, wakey, rise and shine!' he bawled. We didn't require much waking. It had been an awful first night at sea. 'Gosh! Why didn't I join the Army or even the Air Force?' I groaned to myself. All of us had spent the terrible night heaving up on the deck below the glutinous meal we had scoffed some hours before.

'Out of it, out of it!' said LS Starkey, poking each hammock with a stick. 'You can get this bloomin' mess cleaned up as soon as you like! You'll find buckets and scrubbers in the 'eads, so let's be 'aving you!' Between the moans and groans we made the effort to do as he asked. Later, reasonably satisfied, he bellowed, 'I've a cure for you lot – follow me!'

We followed him along alleyways and stairways, stepping over bodies that had long given in to empty stomachs! At last we emerged on to the open deck. The North Atlantic in January was, for us, a sight to behold!

'Follow me!' he roared, adding, 'Hold on to the handrail!'

We needed no telling to do this, and a very scared bunch of would-be sailors gripped the handrail that ran around the deck housing, hanging on to it for dear life! Hand over hand we followed our wet nurse.

'Far enough!' He uncoiled the line that he carried over his shoulder. 'Stand up straight then!' he roared above the wind and the waves. He passed the rope around each waist, all 20 or so of us, tying it off to the handrail as he passed it round the last waist. We must have been well aft. We watched fascinated, and with some fright – I would be the first to admit that! The stern of the *Andes* seemed to lift out of the Atlantic, and mountains of water passed beneath us as the propellers made a roar like thunder as they lifted clear of the sea. Grey skies and grey mountains seemed to come charging at us as we stood tied to the handrail. Above it all, he roared, 'I'll be back in an hour to see how you all are!' and he was off, leaving us to it!

Even in my state, I looked up at the DEMS gunners, well wrapped up in their duffel coats, looking down at us with a bit of a grin on their faces, as they watched the scene being played out below them! 'You'll be better for some fresh air inside you,' he had said...

Miracles do sometimes happen. For me and for most of us, one happened as we were tied up to that handrail. I couldn't believe it when I found myself feeling better and losing that empty horrible feeling in my stomach that had been with me all night and most of the morning. Thankfully it was going, as I felt the warmth and colour come flooding back to my face. No doubt about it, I was starting to feel my sea legs, that was for sure.

Old Starkey was back, as promised, an hour later and untied us. Half an hour later we found our way below and, as if we owned the place, strolled in into an almost empty dining hall and scoffed as much breakfast as we liked!

We found a little time to pity the less unfortunate who hadn't such a wise old wet nurse as we had!

Little ole New York

'Prepare to disembark at 1400 hours!' the voice announced over the tannoy. We had packed up our kit bags, tied up our hammocks and went on deck to get a first view of the USA. Everybody had the same idea, but we found ourselves a spot on A deck, portside, to get a grandstand view.

The captain had been right about the weather; from the gales of the first few days, the sea was now calm, and it was a still, misty morning as the *Andes* edged her way into the Hudson River. We caught a glimpse of the Statue of Liberty as it gleamed white above the low-lying mist. Then, slowly above the mist the Manhattan skyline emerged. Excited and eager we 'oohed' and 'aahed' as we viewed the most famous skyline in the world. The sea sickness of the previous days was now forgotten as we recognised each famous landmark that previously we had only seen on the pictures!

'Cor, look at that – it's the Empire State Building. It's the tallest building in the world! And we gave it our full attention until somebody pointed out another 'wonder' to gawp at!

'Look, there's one of the "Queens" – it's the "Mary",' said a know-all, 'cos it's got three stacks!' I felt proud, because for all the fabulous buildings New York could boast, amongst it all here was a little bit of Old England taking Yankee troops back to the UK. 'Fair exchange, no robbery!' I thought. As the tugs shepherded the *Queen Mary* out from under Brooklyn Bridge she gave three mighty blasts on her sirens. I felt my chest expand another inch!

Two hours later, kit bag over my shoulder, hammock under my arm, I walked down the gangway of the *Andes* into Brooklyn Navy Yard. With my feet now firmly on good old 'terra firma', I was a sailor that I knew would never be sea sick again!

'I knew I would never be seasick again.'

Asbury Park, New Jersey

It was night-time when we arrived at Asbury Park, 60 or so miles down the coast from New York. The train from Grand Central Station took us under the Hudson River and down the Atlantic coast. It had been a fine winter's day when we left New York but as we got off the train and unloaded our belongings, a light covering of snow was on the ground. We piled our kit on to the lorry. Two lads hopped inside, pleased that they had escaped the march to our 'billets'.

'Right-oh, lads, get fell in!'

'We ought to 'ave got our overcoats on!' the cry went up.

'Overcoats, overcoats, what are we, men or mice? Step it out and show 'em the Royal Navy's in town. Right, left, right!' came the cry as he followed behind.

A young girl, well wrapped up with her dog, and a bemused-looking station master watched us swing out over the railway lines, 'Left, right, left, right', as the snow came down heavier. Our billets turned out to be what had once been a swanky hotel on the sea front. The foyer was full of boarded-up one-armed bandits and juke-boxes! I had a top bunk in a bedroom next to a tall window. Lying there I was able to view the bright lights that stretched out for miles. No blackout blinds or curtains, just sparkling lights, a

scene that I had forgotten ever existed! For a while I lay there, listening to that wailing, moaning sound as the trains went through Asbury Park Station, so unlike the old familiar whistles of our trains back home!

I wondered how they were back home. Bob and Chris may be married now! I had mastered the seasickness of eight to ten days ago, but, right now, another sickness was creeping up on me. I was homesick.

There was little else to do as we waited for the next move. One Sunday morning four of us ventured along the 'boardwalk'. It was a cold blustery Sunday morning in January. The Atlantic came rolling in across the empty beaches towards deserted, boarded-up little gift shops and upturned boats. 'Gee!' I thought. 'It's just like Southend on a wet Sunday in February!'

We forgot the weather, forgot 'home sweet home' and rendered, for the locals, four verses of 'Roll me over in the clover'!

We could expect, the 'Subby' said, to be here another 14 days, then it was off to Vancouver in British Columbia, four to five days' train journey across the States! In the meantime, one day's leave would be granted for a trip back to New York. We were paid in US dollars, and with our pay books lined with these, we set off on a whole day's leave in New York!

On ole Broadway

'Where's this Stage Door Canteen of yours?'

We marvelled at the marble walls in Grand Central Station, marvelled at all the goodies in the shops and big stores, took in all the sights along Broadway and Fifth Avenue, compared Central Park with Hyde Park, took the elevator to the top of the Empire State, free of course, and found space to carve our initials amongst the many hundreds who had left their mark before us, and managed a free beer in Jack Dempsey's famous bar on Broadway.

We stopped for a breather opposite the theatre where *Oklahoma!* had just opened and watched the moving sign with all the latest war news.

''ere!' said Charlie. 'I'm going to 'ave a laugh with this cop!' Charlie was Poplar born and bred and could turn on his rich Cockney accent when he felt inclined. 'Er, mate, where's this 'ere Stage Door Canteen of yours?' he asked the burly New York city policeman.

He eyed Charlie and the rest of us up and down and pointed, saying, 'Ten blocks down the Avenue "mate", that's if your "plates of meat" will get you that far!' Our Charlie looked as if he hoped that the ground under New York would open up and swallow him! His joke had misfired!

'OK, sailors,' said the policeman. 'I'll let on – my dear old Mum and Dad came from your London's East End, way back in the early '20s and us kids were in stitches as they talked between themselves in their best Cockney rhyming slang. Apples and pears, tit for tat, whistle and flute – me and my sister have never forgotten it. My sister has a book full of it! She lives down in Philly.'

'Philly?' we all asked.

'Yeah, Philadelphia. They're all posh down there,' and with a broad smile added, 'That's where they speak proper English! Now, this Stage Door Canteen you're looking for. You've a long walk, mates. Our patrol car will be along in five minutes. I'll ask the guys to give you a lift down there!'

We climbed into the back seat, and as we did so thanked our copper mate!

On arrival they said, 'You'll have a long wait if you get in that queue, sailors – it goes around three blocks!' We agreed and slowly made our way back up Fifth Avenue.

'Hiya, limeys!' said a passer-by, stopping us. 'How they doing over there? What do you think of our little ole town? I was over there in 1917 – we gave them what for then and we'll do it again!' He stopped for breath, then went on. 'This is our front-line city, you know.' We looked at each other and put our hands over our mouths to hide our grins! 'Yeah,' he said, 'we often hear explosions out there!' He pointed to goodness knows where!

It was a fact, we were later to learn, that as the Battle of the Atlantic swung in the Allies' favour, Hitler's U-boats left the mid-Atlantic, where they had ruled the roost for so long, our very existence tottering on a knife-edge in those days. They now hunted off the US East Coast, picking off lone oil tankers as they came up from the Gulf of Mexico before joining an eastbound convoy off New York. Front-line city, though? Hardly that, I thought, when in my mind I saw the rubble and chaos in the bombed-out streets of my old home town, dear old E13.

They talked a lot, did New Yorkers, but they were kind and generous to us. Before our friend rushed off, he pushed a 5-dollar bill into each of our hands. 'Have a drink on me, fellas.' He left us to it and disappeared into the crowds!

Exhausted from the day's excitement, I lay on my bunk looking out of the window at the twinkling lights of Asbury Park. 'Gosh!' I thought. 'It's so unfair, me here enjoying all the sights and big eats, while Mum and everybody back home live on rationing and struggle through the blackout, never knowing from one day to the next what other horrible tricks old Hitler has up his sleeve!'

Of course, that lousy homesickness crept up on me from time to time. I wished old Stripey was around with another of his magic cures! I turned away from the twinkling lights, pulled the blanket up over my shoulders and dreamed of 'home sweet home'!

Way out West

'When it's springtime in the Rockies!'

We had little to do and the last 14 days at Asbury Park dragged by. In the forenoons we swept and polished in the usual 'Andrew' manner. 'Make and Mends' were piped after the midday meal. It was with relief that we were told to pack up as we would be on our way again in two days; we were given our forwarding address to send home. I remembered the kind, silver-haired ladies in the local servicemen's clubs who offered to write home merely to say that, 'Your son, Kenneth Kimberley, visited us here today and we can let you know that he is fit and well.' They even cajoled us into sending a recorded message home.

'Pop into the booth,' said one lady, 'and when the red light comes on start to speak.'

'What about my tip, sailors?'

With a few 'ers' and 'ahs' I managed to say something!

'I'll play it back for you,' she said.

'Was that me talking?' I asked her.

We boarded the giant train at Newark, New Jersey. It was the biggest train you ever saw. We settled down, four at a time, in the luxurious compartments. The well-upholstered seats served as our bunks at night. It was all posh, the tiny hand basins concealed in the rich wood panelling and hidden lighting throwing a soft rosy light over everything. This is the life, we all agreed.

The Transit Officer came into the compartment and read the Riot Act of 'Dos and Don'ts'. He said we would be stopping at Pittsburgh, Chicago, St Paul, Minneapolis, Calgary in the Rockies, then on to Vancouver in British Columbia. It would take four days. 'I don't have to remind you that US Navy and Army patrols will be vigilant at all exits!'

Being flat broke after our trip into New York, I don't think anybody had the inclination to scarper, as we were three thousand miles away from home. However, I did manage to rustle up a few cents to buy postcard views of each city at every stop on the way.

Our 'Rochester', with his big beaming smile, white jacket and broom, was forever saying, 'You sailor boys, are you, OK?' On the first day, while we had our evening meal in the luxury dining car, he turned our seats into beds. 'What about my tip, sailors?' he asked, holding out his hand.

'We're all broke,' we said.

The big smile left his face and we didn't see much of him after that...

We crossed the great Mississippi River and the next day the giant train started its climb up into the Rocky Mountains. 'When it's springtime in the Rockies' we all sang, accompanied by Willy on his mouth-organ. I thought of the old Southend-on-Sea excursion – it was never anything like this! There cannot be grander, more majestic scenery in the whole wide world, with waterfalls falling into deep ravines amongst boulders and dense pine forests, as the giant engine pulled the train across tall wooden bridges. The line went on for mile after mile, alongside great lakes and past snow-covered mountains. Everywhere we looked reminded us of glorious Technicolor pictures. No wonder old Bob used to write home about it all in such glowing terms.

On arrival we climbed the gangway of the depot aircraft carrier. The hanger deck was filled with bunk beds. I claimed an empty one and sat down on it. So this ship, or something like it, was to be my home for the foreseeable future!

Commissioning CVE 51

Apple-pie, ice-cream and Chinese laundries!

It was early springtime in Vancouver. Most of the draft that had left the UK and travelled across the States had commissioned the escort carrier *CVE 50*, and they were out now doing their sea trials. That left a dozen or so, mostly radar lads, to be the advance party on *CVE 51*. The three escort carriers were strung a mile or so apart along the Vancouver waterfront. Stan, our Leading Seaman, Phil and Joe, two Able Seamen and me, the Ordinary Seaman, made up the radar contingent for the time being. The First Lieutenant on the depot carrier was glad to be rid of us, saying, 'Get on board and start tidying up your part of the ship!'

We made our way around all the usual dockyard paraphernalia. Stan, surveying the scene around us, came to the conclusion that it would be months, not weeks, before the *Arbiter* would be ready for her sea trials!

Right opposite our berth on the waterfront was an appetising-looking diner, wedged between a barber's shop and a Chinese laundry. Vancouver had a large Chinese population, and each one, we thought, owned a laundry! After 'tidying up' each day on board, the inevitable happened. We thought we would see what the diner had to offer. Pushing a nickel or a dime into the juke-box, we sat perched on the stools at the counter and enjoyed the best apple-pie and ice-cream you ever tasted! We took it in turns to act as lookout, just in cast the 'Jimmy' came up from the depot carrier, snooping about to see what we were up to!

'Oh, crikey!' Stan said. 'Old Phil's up on the flight deck waving to us like mad. Come on! It must be the "Jimmy" on his way!' We left our half-finished apple-pie and scarpered across to the ship.

I bet old Taff Jenkins up in North Wales would have stood over me and said, ''Course, it would have to be you!', because as I chased after the others I ran full tilt into a little Chinese carrying a basket full of newly laundered washing! It spilled out everywhere and I, in a panic, hastily endeavoured to put everything back in his basket, doing my best to brush off all the bits and pieces of gravel that the washing had picked up on the roadway! It was a good job I couldn't understand a word he was going on about – I bet it would have made any Liverpool docker blush!

'Sorry,' I gasped as I gathered up the last piece. There was no time for any more apologies as I bounded up the gangway after the others!

'Everything all right, lads?' the 'Jimmy' asked us as he saw us busy with our buckets and brooms…

Each day *CVE 51* became more shipshape, and more and more crew arrived. Came the day, *Arbiter* had her full complement of seamen, stokers, bunting tossers, sparks, cooks and ten or so radar ratings, POs, CPOs – and there was plenty of gold braid about too!

The 'ditch' at Panama
'Clear the upper decks now!'

The *Arbiter* had been built, along with the other escort carriers, down the West Coast of America in Seattle. Prefabricated and welded together bit by bit, it was a job to find a nut, bolt or rivet anywhere! There were bunk beds throughout (goodbye hammocks) and no galley messing, as was the case in all RN ships, but cafeteria catering instead. The wooden flight deck was no bigger that a matchbox, some said, and Bofors guns lined the port and starboard catwalks, with two 4-inch guns, one aft and one on the quarter deck.

There was a steam catapult, aircraft lifts, one forward and one aft, and a radar 'SK' aircraft-warning aerial high above the bridge – we nicknamed it 'the bedstead' because that's what it looked like. Lower down was the 'SG' surface-warning radar aerial, both operated from our radar cabin alongside the 'ops' room, housed below the flight deck. We had a canteen and a canteen flat, and a ship's laundry too!

As the *Arbiter* left her berth special sea duty men were piped to their stations for the first time. I wasn't on watch, so, out of view of the bridge, me and my mates took one last look at Vancouver with the majestic Rockies towering up behind the city. We remembered Stanley Park with its Indian totem poles and giant trees and, of course, our favourite diner, the barber's shop and the Chinese laundry next door. There they were, outside their shops, giving us a send off; Big Bill stood on his step, the little Chinese people waved like mad, and the barber waved his apron, and we all waved back to them.

We did the customary sea trials in Vancouver Bay – speed trials, practice gunnery shoots, radar tracking runs with a Royal Canadian Navy destroyer – then the day came when the first aircraft squadron landed one by one on our small flight deck. At last it seemed that the ship was fully operational. As the Rockies and lovely Vancouver Bay disappeared aft, we all realised that this was the first leg of the long journey back to the UK.

Fifteen hundred miles or so later we tied up alongside in San Diego, California, and refuelled. Twenty Chief Petty Officers were invited up to Hollywood for a sight-seeing trip! Lucky blokes!

A further three thousand miles south we were issued with the standard RN tropical kit: white shorts and black knee-length stockings. The same day the ship went alongside in Panama City. We dug deep into our pockets for the last dime and nickel – the ship's company was broke after runs ashore in Vancouver – and treated ourselves to Panama hats! Waiting there to go into the Canal, our navigator – 'Brains' we called him, the most popular officer on the ship after the 'Jimmy' – gave us, over the tannoy, a short history of the waterway.

Apparently the 'ditch' was opened to shipping in 1914, ten years after the digging out started. The side walls of the locks were 45 feet thick at the base, tapering up to 10 feet thick at the top, which could be seen above the lock's waterline.

Initially thousands of lives were lost through yellow fever and malaria, and it was here that mosquitoes were discovered to carry these deadly diseases. At the time it was the most disease-ridden place on earth! Many, many corporations went bankrupt building the canal, then finally Theodore Roosevelt's Government took over the whole project, and the finished result we were to see over the next few days. The final cost was $380 million! Old 'Brains' had certainly done his homework on the 'ditch'!

It was fascinating to watch the electric mules pull us into each lock as we neared the end of the Canal. We were now on the Atlantic side, 60 feet higher than the Pacific Ocean end. We were all sporting our Panama hats up on the flight

deck and catwalks and the new Officer of the Watch, spotting this, piped, 'Ratings wearing Panama

hats and not the rig of the day, clear the upper decks, *now*!'

'Oh, it's that miserable "wavy navy" bloke up there, miserable old so and so!' we grumbled.

We passed Christobell on the Atlantic side and out into the Caribbean and the weed-strewn Sargasso Sea. Here a stoker turned the wrong wheel, or pulled the wrong knob way down below, and let salt water into the ship's boilers!

A free run ashore

The *Arbiter* dropped anchor in Chesapeake Bay ten hours later, and we went alongside in the US Navy Yard at Newport News, Norfolk, Virginia. The Paymasters also went ashore, hoping to get some pay for us. No such luck! 'Sorry, lads, they've no more money ashore for us!'

Stan, Joe and Phil changed into their No 1s. 'What about you, Kim? Ain't you getting changed?'

'I've no cash.'

They laughed. 'We're all in the same boat. Come on, come ashore and stretch those long legs of yours!'

I changed and went ashore with

'You're all under arrest – this apartment is being used for immoral purposes!'

them. We boarded the ferry, which thankfully was free like the old Woolwich Ferry, and it took us across to Norfolk. We admired the big US Navy battlewagons and carriers as we passed close by.

Two girls sidled up to us as we leaned against the rail.

'Off to see the sights, sailors?' they asked us. Why they picked on us we never knew, because there were plenty of US Navy guys in their summer whites lolling about on deck with us, with, no doubt, loads of cash stashed in their pockets! Stan, as always, was our spokesman.

'Sorry, ladies, we're broke!' he said, indicating his empty pockets.

'That's the last of your worries – you just tag along with us and we'll show you around our little ole town!'

They did that all right. They did us proud. A cinema show, bars and soda fountains, ice-cream parlours – we did it all and at their expense!

'Can anybody cook?' they asked as we all bundled into a cab. They stopped the driver at a food store, coming back with bags of food.

Phil piped up, 'I can cook!'

'There you are, Phil, try this chicken for size!'

We squeezed into the elevator and went up to the apartment. It

was a swanky place with dim lights and posh furniture. We admired the framed photos on the walls showing our two girls in flying suits, climbing up into an American Air Force plane.

'Is that really you?' we asked.

'Sure is! We're ferry pilots – we bring the Navy boys' planes over from the West Coast. We only got in this morning!'

The rich smell of Phil's cooking drifted from the kitchen. Stan looked at his watch, saying, 'Sorry, Kim, you'll have to get back on board.'

They explained to the girls that, being 19, my leave ended at 24.00 hours. They called a cab, paid the driver to take me to the ferry, and, as they did so, each gave me a big kiss! With just ten minutes to spare I walked up the gangway, saluted the side and was handed my station card! I turned in, wondered what was left of the chicken, and fell asleep.

'Come on, come on wake up!'

'What's wrong?' I asked.

'Never mind what's wrong. The Officer of the Day wants to see you on the gangway now!'

I hurried into my No 3s. The Officer's face was as black as thunder.

'Were you ashore with Leading Seaman Harris, Able Seaman Davis

and Able Seaman Thomas yesterday?'

'That's right, sir.'

'Where did you get to?' he asked.

I smiled and told what happened.

'What's up, sir, what's wrong? Where are they?'

'Where are they? he stormed. 'I'll tell you where they are, and count yourself lucky you're not in the b—— local jail with them!'

'Jail, sir? Jail?'

'That's right, b—— jail. They're locked up with two prostitutes! I've got to go and bail them out! We're under sailing orders and I've a good mind to leave them there!'

The duty PO interrupted. 'Better not, sir – they're the best part of the radar team!'

Later Stan explained. 'Shortly after you left and we were sitting down to Phil's chicken there was this hammering on the apartment door. I opened it and was knocked for six by these coppers bursting in, saying, "You're all under arrest – this apartment is being used for immoral purposes!" We did our best to explain that they had it all wrong, but that silly old so and so of an Officer of the Day wouldn't let us open our mouths – all he wanted was to get us back on board.'

Later that afternoon we sailed north to rendezvous with an eastbound convoy off New York.

Back in the war at last

I had the morning watch – 0400/0800 hours – and the scan on the PPI picked up the 'blips' as the ships jostled about to get into five neat lines of ten, 50 in all. We took up our position at the rear of the convoy. It was a busy watch. A thick sea mist enveloped the coast and an anxious Officer of the Watch on the bridge asked for the bearings and ranges of the ships close to us.

'Radar – bridge!'

'Bridge – radar,' he answered 'Ship dead ahead, range 900 yards, closing; ship on port beam, range 1,000 yards, steady; ship on starboard beam, range 1,000 yards, steady.'

I passed these bearings and ranges up to the bridge at 2-minute intervals, in between the scan's all-round sweeps. And that's how the 4 hours passed on my first watch in convoy!

'Dawn Action Stations' sounded during the watch and, as daylight came up, a relieved Officer of the Watch called, 'We have perfect visibility now, radar – carry on with your normal sweeps!' I knew that he was a young 'Subby', and like me probably doing his first watch doing the real thing!

I passed over my watch and hurried off to the galley to see what was on for breakfast. To do this I stepped out on to the catwalk. I had by now, together with the other lads, perfected a quick ride down the ladder, with hands on rail and ankles cocked over it. In this fashion I slid with ease down the smooth handrail.

It was now clear and bright. Seaman gunners, standing down from their action stations, were idling about on the catwalk. Others, like me, were off to see what the galley had offer for breakfast. I was pleased with myself, thinking that I had handled my first real watch all right!

I looked about me in awe at the 50 or so merchant ships that moved as one in well-ordered lines, though the one ahead of us was, as it had been while I was on watch, still playing up a bit! Oil tankers, long and low in the water, were taking their precious cargoes back to the UK. Ships that had seen better days, with their tall spindly funnels, plodded along with the Liberty ships that had come out of the Seattle yards, like we had, their squat low funnels making them instantly recognisable, together with their life-rafts fore and aft, angled for a speedy release, and the gun platforms mounted on the fo'c'sle and quarter decks. Low down on the horizon were the DEs, their bow waves visible rushing down their sides.

I was exhilarated to feel a part of it all! I could clearly see on to a DE's bridge as it came between us and a merchantman and I heard the conservation that passed between them over their loud hailers.

'DE to *Empire Warrior*. What are you burning? The old man's socks, cos you're making smoke!'

'*Empire Warrior* to DE. This is the old man in his socks. B—— off!'

'DE to *Empire Warrior*. Your wish is our command!'

With that the DE charged down the lane like a greyhound, bullying the ship ahead of us to get back on station!

Coming in on a wing and a prayer

We dropped behind the convoy and turned into the wind, while a lone destroyer took up position astern of us. We were in mid-Atlantic and one by one the aircraft took off and did their routine patrols. An anxious Commander 'F' in the Ops room adjacent to our radar cabin waited for their return. One came in fair and square, the arrester wire catching him perfectly. As his boots touched the flight deck the pilot gave the bridge a thumbs-up sign!

Not so the next kite. The flight deck gave a sudden lurch to port at the vital moment, and the pilot missed the wire and skidded down the flight deck, smoke from the tyres scorching the deck. The aircraft carried on, its port wing cutting through anything that came in its way, as the gun crew and bystanders dived for cover beneath the overhanging flight deck. Eventually it stopped and hung there, precariously balanced over the catwalk. The flight-deck crew hung on to it for all their worth as the pilot scrambled to safety!

The next one was not so fortunate. He also missed the arrester wire as the deck again dipped down at the wrong time, and unable to stop on the short flight deck, he took off, only to plunge over the fo'c'sle and into the 'oggin'. The watching flight-deck crew rushed to the side as the Avenger rode on the waves down the port side.

'There he is, there he is!' someone shouted, pointing out the pilot's head and shoulders on the crest of a wave. They watched as the DE rushed up alongside the *Arbiter*, and as we quickly drew away we were unable to see the outcome…

We arrived in Liverpool Bay with a severely depleted squadron.

Be served by the stars

We joined the queue outside the Stage Door Canteen and moved slowly towards the flag-bedecked entrance. One of our number said that the last time he was here, 'Betty Grable served me with a Coke! I told the missus. "All right for you," she said, "'ere in Bolton, it's blackouts, spam and dried egg, while you live it up in New York!" She soon quietened down though when I gave her two pairs of silk stockings! "When you going back?" she asked me!'

'Be served by the Stars' the notice said. We missed out on the stars that day, but we could stick out or chests and say, 'We finally made it into the Stage Door Canteen!

On the trip back the Captain announced that, 'Under the supreme command of General Eisenhower, Allied Forces early today have made successful landings in Normandy!'

There was wild cheering at this news, the older hands saying, 'And about b—— time!'

Liverpool – so near and yet so far

This time around we missed the bar tide in Liverpool, which meant dropping the 'hook' and spending the night in Liverpool Bay. And the fo'c'sle party were horrified early in the forenoon watch the following day when their endeavours to raise the anchor failed. There were buzzes going about the lower deck that when we did get alongside in Liverpool, each watch would be getting three days leave down the 'smoke'.

A naval tug with a diver on board came alongside. He had a large audience as preparations were made for him to go down and find out what had happened to our hook.

'Want to borrow our Buffer's 'acksaw?' somebody called out.

The anchor was fouled up with an unmarked wreck, we were told. Two days later a relieved fo'c'sle party raised the anchor, and our boiler clean having been thrown into complete disarray, leave was cancelled.

Back in Norfolk we wondered how our two 'girl friends' of the previous visit were faring! This time on our return we didn't unload our cargo of planes in Liverpool, but at some obscure landing stage on the River Clyde, between Greenock and Glasgow. We mustered in the now-empty hangar deck.

'Well, men,' the skipper told us, 'I've to tell you that our Atlantic days are over. The port watch will proceed on seven days leave as from 0100 hours tomorrow. The duty watch on board will take the ship across to Belfast, where the port watch will rejoin. They will rejoin the ship in Harland & Wolff's yards where a major refit will be carried out. That is all! Dismiss the ship's company, No 1.'

There was a buzz of excitement as the First Lieutenant dismissed us, and concern from the older hands.

'What's the refit all about?' they asked.

'Who cares?' us younger ones asked. This time tomorrow we would be down the 'smoke'!

For the first time in months, sacks full of mail came on board. I got my share, ten letters in all, mostly from Mum. Her letters said that Bob and Christine married in February. Jimmy McNeil, Bob's navigator, was their best man. She did them proud it seems, considering how difficult things were in wartime. Everybody, including half the street, had a whale of a time! There was a letter from dear Aunt Liz, saying that my cousin Billy was on a destroyer based at Gibraltar, one from Aunt Pearl, with its customary 10 shilling postal order, bless her, one from Uncle Jim, and another from the old firm, Butler & Crisp, down at Clerkenwell!

The last letter had me guessing. I recognised my last letter to Bob. 'Strange,' I thought, 'that it should be returned to me.' On the envelope it said 'Return to Sender, c/o GPO London.'

'Oh, he's been posted to another station, perhaps abroad,' I thought, as I stuffed all the letters in my locker and prepared for the big day tomorrow – I was in the port watch.

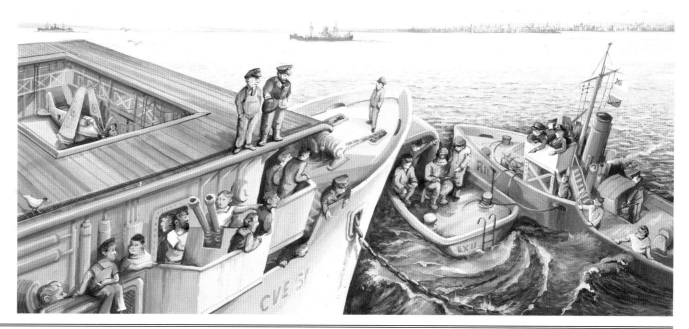

Seven days down the line

We had a few hours in Glasgow, enabling us to stock up with some bottles of beer – of course, we were all well off with our duty frees!

We were in a buoyant and happy mood when we sorted ourselves out on the Euston-bound train. As ever the compartment became hot and stuffy and wreathed in fag smoke. For the hundredth time I checked that my leave pass, travel warrant, ration card and pay book were safely tucked up inside my jumper! I glanced up to see that my suitcase, with all of its precious 'rabbits' packed inside, was all right amongst the other cases on the rack above!

Funny, I thought again, about my letter to Bob being returned. I remembered his previous letter to me, saying how he was now settled down with Chris in a cottage in Lincolnshire, near the aerodrome at Northcotes. He wrote how happy they both were, and at the same time how busy he was. I was in do doubt what these last few lines referred to!

They were all right at home too. Mum's letter had said that Hitler's buzz bombs had so far left Brooklands Gardens alone. What with my seven days leave now here, everything looked 'hunky-dory'. Satisfied with these thoughts I dozed off with the rest of them.

One of the lads was on his feet as we drew into Crewe Station. 'I'm dying for a cup of tea,' he said, as he went out into the corridor.

'Silly blighter,' I thought, as I saw him disappear into the refreshment room. 'We might only be here for a few minutes.' The clock above the platform read 2.30am.

Moments later he came charging out through the refreshment room doors, a cup of something held in each hand. I opened the corridor door for him, but it was too late – with jolts and jerks we were on our way to Euston! I saw him in his haste trip over the luggage trolley handle. 'No way back for him now,' I thought.

'We'll leave your stuff in the left luggage office at Euston,' I yelled

out, and with a wave we left him sitting on the platform with his cup of tea! I did as promised and left his case and cap in the left luggage office.

We walked out under the Euston Arch, went around the square and down the Euston Road to the underground. The familiar Inner Circle train took us to Liverpool Street where we stood under the old clock and said our goodbyes: 'See you in seven days.' Then we were off on our separate ways.

For the first time in nearly 12 months I stood alone. I couldn't believe the quiet around me after all of the mess-deck chatter of the last year! I looked up at the clock, still there after all the bombing of the previous years. A quarter to five, it read.

'The first one out to Romford is 5.20,' I was told. The NAAFI's up there in the corner, jack. It never closes!'

It was unfair of me to compare it with all of those swanky US servicemen's clubs that I had got used to. No doubt about it, I had been spoiled! The not-so-hot cup of tea and yesterday's-looking spam sandwich said it all. Who cared, though, in just a few more hours I would be home!

I boarded the No 66 outside the station, offering the conductor my fare. 'That's all right, jack,' he said, ''ave it on London Transport.'

Halfway home, I couldn't resist the urge to get off and enjoy the walk for the rest of the way! It was light now, and early risers were hurrying to the station to get the 'Workmen's'.

'Any buzz bombs been about?' I asked the conductor as I got off with my suitcase.

'Er, yes, there was one near Slewins Lane a few days ago,' he said.

That worried me because it would be close to home.

''ave a good leave, jack,' he said as he ding-dinged the bell. The 66 went off up Victoria Road.

With my suitcase full of its precious 'rabbits' I stepped out. When I opened the gate I noticed the boarded-up window in the bay and spotted the broken roof tiles in the flower border that lined the path.

'This will be a nice surprise for Mum,' I thought. There had been no time to let her know of my leave.

I lifted the knocker and let it drop. Paddy gave his customary bark of old. It was Chris who opened the door. I was surprised to see her as I thought she was with Bob up at Northcotes.

She looked tired and worn out, nothing like the bubbly, laughing girl that I remembered standing on the steps with Bob at the Pwllheli Arms Hotel just 12 months ago.

'Bob's missing,' she said.

I remembered his previous letter to me...

'I walked under Euston Arch
and around the square.'

'The Inner Circle train took
me to Liverpool Street.'

'I knocked at the door… "Bob's missing," Chris said.'

Looking for Bob

Mum came from the kitchen, looking as Chris did. I had never seen such anxiety on her face. She put on a smile when she said, 'I didn't expect to see you, Ken.'

I explained that there had been no time to let her know of my leave.

'I'll put the kettle on. You must be starving – I'll make you some breakfast!'

I sat at the table, thinking that the unthinkable had happened. Bob had always ended his letters to me, 'Never ever worry about me, kid, come what may I'll always get home. When this b—— nuisance of a war is over we'll make up for all the lost time!'

He was so confident about it all coming right for us in the end. As I sat there I glimpsed my suitcase standing in the hall, the little surprises it contained for them all now forgotten.

Chris said that it was a Sunday afternoon when she heard the Beaufighter squadron take off. She had got used to the routine, living so near the 'drome. 'He'll be back about nine,' she had thought.

However, it wasn't Bob who wheeled his bike into the backyard of the cottage. It was a kindly WAAF, who had come to tell Chris the news that all servicemen's wives, mothers, fathers, brothers, sisters and sweethearts feared one day that they may hear.

A few days later Mum had travelled to Northcotes to bring Chris home, along with Dizzy Bon the cat, Bob's bike and his few possessions.

Later that evening Uncle Jim called in with a copy of the *Daily Telegraph* (he worked for the *Telegraph* up in Fleet Street). He was surprised to see me. He handed me the paper in which the report read:

'Beaufighters of Coastal Command on Sunday last attacked, with rocket-fired missiles and cannon fire, a formation of enemy naval vessels off the Dutch Coast. Two of them sank, and three others left ablaze. One Beaufighter bomber is missing.'

'Look,' Uncle Jim said, 'call in at the office tomorrow morning and I'll have ready a list of bureaux that seek out news of prisoners-of-war and missing personnel.' We thanked him and agreed to do as he suggested.

Later that night I thought of the crazy, barmy hours that I and my mates had spent swaggering around New York, scoffing down T-bone steaks, ice-cream and apple-pie. Just 14 days ago I was checking to see if my initials were still there at the top of the Empire State Building. While we were up to these antics, 3,000 miles away Bob with his pals in the air, and thousands on the ground, were being shot at and shot down.

I remembered Uncle George, Mum's brother, who had gone to France in 1915. 'Missing' they said he was. Uncle George was never seen or heard of again. Our Dad survived a gas attack, but was to die when Bob and me were both very young, from a lung disease brought on by poison gas, so they said. And now Bob was missing, just like Uncle George. Mr Murray, our teacher down at Balaam Street, used to lecture us on the horrors and futility of war – how right he was!

I couldn't sleep that night. I was feeling full of guilt and remorse.

Next day I guided Chris across

'Can you give me your husband's full name…?'

busy Fleet Street to collect Uncle Jim's list. As I did so I spotted the telegram boy on his red bike. I wondered what good or bad news he was about to deliver.

The silver-haired lady said, 'Do please sit down.' Chris sat down opposite her at the desk, and I stood behind her.

She reached for a pen and pad.

'Can you give me your husband's full name, service number and rank?'

Chris did so in a firm clear voice.

This was to be the pattern of the next few hours as we left Bob's

details at four or so different addresses in the West End.

'Thank you, Mrs Kimberley. As soon as we have news of your husband's whereabouts, and any

news that is forthcoming, we will inform you immediately. Goodbye.'

'Well, Mum and Chris, we've done all we can. We must be patient, pray and keep our fingers crossed!'

The Belfast refit

We found her high and dry in dry dock.

I walked under the Arch at Euston, remembering how a few days before I had been full of the joys of spring with my case full of 'rabbits'! With the other lads I read the notice at the barrier that said all *Arbiter* ratings should report to the RTO. We handed in our travel warrants for Glasgow and new ones were issued for Stranraer. A few hours later we sat on the Euston-Stranraer train.

The journey seemed never-ending, as all train journeys did in those times. The compartment soon filled with the customary fag smoke and empty bottles. I couldn't join in the usual backchat and banter that was the norm on such journeys. I

'With the other lads I read the notice at the barrier.'

sat there, with my thoughts on Bob, Mum and Chris.

Almost a day later we made our way around all the normal dockyard odds and ends. It had been raining and it all looked dark, wet and miserable – just as I felt! Through the partly opened doors of the Harland & Wolff workshops I saw blokes hard at it on their night shifts. They didn't seem very concerned at blackout rules and regulations.

We eventually found the *Arbiter*, high and dry in dry dock. As we neared the gangway, we could see the starboard watch all dressed up in their No 1s, suitcases and bags at the ready for their seven days leave.

'You've 'ad it, mates – what's it like coming back?' It was all the usual banter, but I felt in no mood to join in. 'Oh, get stuffed,' I thought.

It was a sad O/S Kimberley who got out of his No 1s and changed into his No 3s. I opened my locker door and as I did so all the letters that I had stuffed so hurriedly into it some seven days ago fell out on to the deck. I picked them up, along with the one that had been returned to me from Northcotes. The mystery was solved. No wonder it had been sent back, I thought.

Northern Ireland being Northern Ireland, the 'Jimmy' posted sentries

all round the ship. I was on familiar ground, since my rounds took in the radar cabin and the Ops room. I made myself at home in the radar mechanics' cubby-hole. The dreary monotonous hours and days passed by. The daytime echoed to the din and chatter of the Irish dockyard maties. They were a good crowd, always finding the time to have a laugh and a joke. I handed around my duty frees, and in return they left me their daily newspapers when they knocked off for the day.

It was a major refit. Brand-new radar equipment was installed in our radar cabin and the operations room. New ventilation trunking lined the bulkheads in the mess decks and part of the bridge was covered in. It seemed that the starboard watch's buzz that we were 'going out East' became more likely every day. I wearied of the dreary routine, but one day I eyed the bench in my cubby-hole and had a brainwave!

My Irish mates brought me in bits and pieces of wood. They even lent me a chisel, a few in fact, along with a hammer. When I wasn't doing the rounds I set about shaping the bits of wood, held firmly in the vice on the bench.

The hours passed more quickly now as the bits of wood took on the shape of the ship's hull. The

Golden Hind it was to be, I decided.

'Good for you, boyo,' the

shipyard workers said as they popped in to see the progress. 'You could do with a bit of sandpaper. You've done this before, I bet.' I had, in the little boxroom in Khartoum Road E13, where Bob and me spent hours making bits and pieces for our model railway before the war!

Mum's letters came regularly. 'No news of our Bob,' she would always end…

I wrote back to Mum saying, 'Keep your chin up, time is still young.' But I realised that with each passing week time was slipping away for any news of Bob's survival.

Meanwhile the foreman stood back and admired the finished hull of my *Golden Hind*. He bent down to get a closer look and with a wink said, 'You'll be leaving the yard in three weeks time, for sea trials out in the lough, boyo.'

The refit was nearing completion. We said that if you stood still long enough, you would get a coat of paint with everything else! The ship's complement was increased, and many of the original crew that commissioned in Vancouver had been drafted elsewhere during the refit.

The day came when we left the dry dock and berthed elsewhere. Our sentry duties were no longer necessary so I put the *Golden Hind* on top of my locker to finish off some other time and some other place!

The sea trials were completed in Belfast Lough. A squadron came on board, just as one had done all those months before off Vancouver. I wrote a last letter home, asking Mum not to worry, that no news was good news about Bob.

With our destroyer escort we rounded the northern tip of Ireland, and I saw on the SG radar the outline of Rathlin Island off the port bow, and the Mull of Kintyre off the starboard quarter. We left the North Channel and sailed due south and not west as we had done in the past. The weather was good as we crossed the Bay of Biscay.

Our new skipper was determined to use every waking hour to bring the *Arbiter* up to its full operational potential.

In Gibraltar the real hard graft started. Nobody was spared, except those on watch as we lay alongside. We all mucked in with the seamen. Sides of beef, sack after sack of flour, cases of this, cases of that, were all manhandled down to the canteen flat. Us radar lads were on the quay, loading up the rope nets with ammo boxes, which in turn were winched up to the flight deck. Two long days we were at it. We sang 'Praise the Lord and pass the ammunition' as each loaded net was hoisted up above us.

Special sea-duty men were piped, then we headed east through the Med.

The Med

The Rock fell astern, and I remembered Aunt Liz's letter saying that my cousin Billy Wilkins was on a destroyer based at Gibraltar. It brought back memories of our childhood days together, when on a miserable Monday washday morning, if it was raining, and we wailed 'What can we do?'

Driving her patience to the limits, Aunt Liz gave us two of Uncle Bill's tack hammers and a tin full of tin tacks, then sat us down by the wooden backdoor step, saying, 'There you are, that'll give you something to do!'

Some hours later Aunt Liz had a door step full of tin tacks! I wondered if they were still there.

I suppose this same 'What can we do?' problem found us up on the flight deck. Off watch, time hung heavily on our hands. With dhobying done, and all the other mundane jobs finished, there was little to do.

'I've got a tennis ball, so what about a kick-about?'

We needed no second asking as we kicked the ball around between the parked planes, out of view of the bridge I might add. Of course, it got more boisterous the longer it went on. As I lay sprawled out on the deck I saw a pair of legs beneath the belly of a kite making their way towards us. The trousers had creases in them! Too late for us, he came round the nose of the Avenger.

'Oh, crikey, it's Commander 'F'!'

Commander Flying was furious. 'Radar people are you? I thought you lot would have had more sense. Who's the leading hand?' he asked.

There wasn't one because we were all ODs.

'I've a good mind to have you all

We stood in silence for a minute.

up in front of the Captain. Don't you realise the damage you could have done to my planes?'

With this, he picked up our tennis ball and hurled it into the Med! A thousand miles further on 'Off-watch ratings muster on the forward lift' was piped.

Our new Captain brought on board a great reputation. He had commanded with distinction one of the cruisers that had sealed the *Graf Spee*'s fate at the River Plate. He had performed heroics in the dark days of the Battle of the Atlantic, and right here in the Med. He addressed us, saying 'The navigator informs me that at this very moment the island of Malta is 100 miles off our port bow, Tripoli in North Africa is off our starboard quarter. I ask you all to stand with me in silence for one minute as a salute to all of or comrades who gave up their lives in defence of the island of Malta. Royal Navy and Merchant Navy seamen alike stood shoulder to shoulder to keep the supply line open for those brave Maltese people.

'Let us not forget too, the gallant men of the 8th Army who freed North Africa of the German Afrika Korps.'

We stood there in silence and bareheaded for a minute. He then asked us to join him in saying the Lord's Prayer, after which he put his cap back on, the gold braid glistening in the January sunshine.

Suez

We waited for the cruiser to come out so that we could go down the Canal. She went down our port side, pock-marked with shell splinters, a length of her starboard side caved in above the water line. Rusted and worn she was, thanks to the Japanese navy or air force! We were perched up on the flight deck, having nothing better to do.

As we looked across at her, her blokes looked across at us. They gave us what for, in fact more than what for. It was understandable, I expect, they looking across to us, newly refitted, paintwork all fresh. In the time-honoured tradition of the RN, they let us have it, good and proper!

''bout time you got in the war, you've been swinging round the buoy for too long!'

''bout time you got your knees brown. Get some sea-time in!'

These were the more savoury remarks that they yelled across to us; the less savoury ones would be unprintable!

Some of our elders were fed up enough as it was. They felt that they were being shanghaied out East, and you had to sympathise with them. From day one they had given their all on those desperate convoys to Russia and across the Atlantic when everything was in Gerry's favour. Only a few days ago the Skipper and the rest of us stood in silence to give thanks to them. They were now, with us youngsters, bound for another war that they knew little about.

As the ships passed each other, the time-honoured bosun's pipe shrilled out, 'Face the port side and stand to attention!'

'Oh b——!' our elders said with hands in their overall pockets, and as one they marched off across the flight deck.

Thankfully for them a sympathetic Officer of the Watch, who must have witnessed their actions, turned a blind eye to it all. A less sympathetic bloke would certainly have had them up in front of the Captain in the forenoon watch tomorrow!

Trinco'

Twelve hours or so later we turned into the Gulf of Suez, went down into the Red Sea and stood off Aden, which they said was the hottest place on earth! There we were refuelled by a fleet tanker. The rocky barren cliffs of Arabia rose up in the background, a world away from the grandeur of the Rocky Mountains!

Crossing the Indian Ocean, the Skipper had us hard at it, all day and most nights, on exercises and more exercises. He made sure the squadron were also put through their paces.

Seven days later we rounded the southernmost corner of Ceylon, and sailed due north to Trincomalee, or Trinco' as the Far East Fleet's anchorage was known throughout the Navy.

'Hands fall in for entering harbour,' was piped. As if it was peacetime, we lined up port and starboard side of the flight deck, with knifelike creases down our shorts.

'Cor,' Charlie muttered to me. 'It ain't 'arf 'ot!

We swung round the buoy, small fry compared to the big boys that had left home waters before us, their war in Europe being over. Charlie said, and I agreed, 'Dunno why they want us with this lot 'ere.'

Each day the ship's motor boat took the Captain ashore. The more knowledgeable elders said, 'He's off again – I bet he's on his knees pleading with 'em ashore to let us get up and at the Japs!'

It was in Trinco' that the sacks of mail came aboard, the first since leaving the UK.

Mum was all right, 'but as yet,' she wrote, 'there's still no news of our Bob.'

Bombay

'What's going on?' we asked ourselves when 50 miles off Cochin on India's south-west coast. The squadron took off and never returned.

The hangar deck was usually a scene of activity, with two lifts continually in use taking kites up and bringing them down for the Fleet Air Arm boys to give them a once over. Now it was quiet and deserted, and we could move about freely without knocking into all the bits and pieces that were usually strewn about everywhere. The Fleet Air Arm boys never took kindly to us when the weather up top was foul and we used the hangar as a means to get from port to starboard!

We discovered why the squadron had taken off and never come back when the Captain cleared the lower deck.

'Looks like we're not wanted here in Trinco',' he said. 'My orders are to proceed to Sydney in Australia, where we'll become part of the newly formed British Pacific Fleet! That is all.'

Bombay was hot and dusty as we wandered about in the midday heat, in and out of the open-fronted bazaars.

'Nice Indian carpet for your cabin, sailor man?' one seller asked us. We fell about laughing at this one.

'Not today, old son,' we told him.

We admired the richly decorated ivory carvings and the array of handsome brassware, all beyond our pockets.

'Mind you, one of those Indian carpets would look 'unky-dory on the deck in the mess!'

''ere,' said Charlie, our Cockney comedian, who had got his come-uppance from that cop in New York, 'I'm going to 'ave a lark with these two blokes.'

We inwardly groaned, but followed our Charlie at a respectable distance to the naval patrol's parked jeep.

''ere mates,' he asked them, 'where's this 'ere Stage Door Canteen you've got 'ere in Bombay? Yer know, like the ones they've got over in the States? We've heard that Bing Crosby, Bob Hope and Dorothy Lamour are 'anding the goodies out there today!'

'Somebody's been pulling your leg, jack,' they replied.

'Pulling me leg?' With that he cocked it up and held it up on the jeep. ''ere,' he said, 'you ain't got much to pull, mate!'

True, we thought, we were always telling him he was a short arse!

'Look lads,' the PO said, 'there's a Union Jack Club of sorts down so and so, down here, down there – it's all right for a glass of beer and a sandwich.'

With that, and shaking their heads, they sped off

Later, back on board, I pictured old Grandad as he opened the atlas on the kitchen table.

'Bombay,' he used to say. 'That's where the ship's going to.'

'What's it like there, Grandad?' we would ask him as we waved to the big ship as it left the docks in Custom House, all those years ago.

Today I had found out for myself.

'Bombay, that's where she's going.'

Crossing the line

War or no war, traditions had to be upheld!

'Does the artist live here?' the Buffer asked as he stepped over the coaming into our mess.

'You want Kim,' I heard them say. 'He's up on his bunk cos he had the middle watch.'

I was lying there awake and I recognised his voice. We were townies, or nearly so. I lived in Hornchurch, and he came from Barking, not too far away! Me and a few others, when off watch, gathered in his locker on the fo'c'sle, where he enjoyed relating his experiences, some true, some imagined, we thought! He should be home tending his garden, but old Hitler put paid to that. Twenty-one years he had been in the RN, and with a few more years under his belt to come, it seemed!

'Oh it's you is it I'm looking for? Look lad, you know we're crossing the line at the end of the week. The Jimmy's asked me to help him with the ceremony.'

The buzz was about that something was on! Tradition dies hard in the RN, none more so that this crossing-the-line thing. War or no war, traditions had to be upheld!

'Look, son, I've got to get these 'ere crossing-the-line scrolls made up. I'm no artist, but I've 'eard you're handy with the brush. Come down to the locker and I'll fix you up with some sail cloth, paint and brushes.'

'Aye aye, Chief – how many do you need?'

'Oh, about two dozen.'

'When?' I asked.

'Soon as you can,' he replied.

He cut out the bits of sailcloth, gave me brushes and paint and an idea of what was wanted, and I set to. I painted on the squares a crude map of the Indian Ocean, with the equator running through the middle. There were sea serpents and other sea monsters leaping about. I enjoyed myself, as it was something to think about and do when off watch. I printed on the top, 'This gallant and brave seaman passed across the equator on this day'. I added a few more mermaids just for luck!

The trouble was that the sailcloth looked just what it was, all limp and not like a rolled-up scroll. The Buffer and I got over that by laying out each one on the flight deck beneath the blazing Indian Ocean sun. We gave them a coat of varnish and they dried before our very eyes – stiff as boards they were. We rolled them up and tied each one with a piece of sail-maker's twine.

The big day came and the fo'c'sle party had rigged up on the fo'c'sle a big tank of sorts filled to overflowing with seawater. It was surrounded on all sides with a raised platform, and a makeshift throne stood at one end (it was a chair nicked from the wardroom for the big occasion). I watched the proceedings from afar, because with lots of my mates I had been a regular in the sick bay for a week or so.

The problem was prickly heat and dhobi rash, which came from not rinsing the pusser's soap out of your underpants. We called him 'Old Iodine' as he painted our middle parts with this foul-smelling, purple-coloured mixture.

'Keep away from salt water at all costs,' he told us.

That was a laugh, since we were surrounded by the stuff night and day!

I watched as each victim got a good old ducking and a scrubbing, and one of my rolled-up scrolls. As each went under I remembered those mouthfuls of carbolicky-tasting water that we endured in the baths at Balaam Street when we were learning to swim. At least old Emmet didn't give us a good scrubbing, like the lads below were enduring!

Off caps and over the side

Some days later we all witnessed a different scene on the fo'c'sle. The off-duty watch, me and the rest stood bareheaded with our caps under our arms. The ship was at a standstill in the southern part of the Indian Ocean. I was looking at the deck and, like the others, not willing to look up at the three lads in their sailcloth shrouds that lay on wood boards. Eventually I glanced up and noticed that our destroyer escort was heaved to, like us, at a respectable distance. Far off a dark rain cloud was emptying itself into the ocean.

'We are gathered here today,' we heard, 'to commit our comrades' bodies to the deep.'

We joined in the Lord's Prayer and singing the hymn, 'For those in peril on the sea'. Then we watched in silence as the sailcloth shrouds were tipped up on the boards and went over the side. We heard the splash below.

''ere,' Charlie said out of the corner of his mouth 'Is that right, Kim? Our Buffer, when he puts the last stitch in the shroud, does he poke the needle through their noses to make sure they're really dead?'

For the first time in his life, Charlie wasn't joking.

Down under

'I bet these Aussie girls will be a bit of all right.'

We lined the flight deck at the usual arm's-length intervals. As we passed under the giant span of Sydney Harbour Bridge it cast what seemed to be a never-ending shadow over us!

''ere, Kim,' Charlie said, as we stood lined up. 'I bet these Aussie girls will be a bit of all right.'

By the looks of things, with lots of waving from the ferries that were zigzagging their way about us, our Charlie could be right! It bode well for the immediate future... Meanwhile, as our anchor went down in Botany Bay, back home they were celebrating VE Day.

The notice on the bar door said 'Males Only – Ladies' Bar Next Door'. We joined an old chap who was on a stool up at the bar.

'Just got in, 'ave you mates?' he asked ''ave a beer with me.'

Aussie hospitality was to prove as generous as that in the US.

Charlie, disappointed at the absence of VE parties and celebrations, had to start the ball rolling. 'Not much in the way of VE celebrations, is there?'

The old chap took the duty free that Charlie offered him. 'Well, it's like this 'ere, mates. A lot of us 'ere didn't look on it as our war, being 12,000 miles away – could you blame us? Mind you, you won't find many of our young blokes walking about Sydney these days. Your old man Churchill saw to that. Where was it they were packed off to – North Africa, Italy, Burma? Don't forget a lot of our

lads were over there in your RAF! I wonder how many of the young b——s will be coming back.'

'Yeah!' answered Charlie, 'but I thought you might be doing a bit of a knees-up to celebrate the end of it!'

'I'm a bit long in the tooth for a knees-up! Fill up their glasses,' he said to the bloke behind the bar, adding, 'We're having a celebration.'

I was relieved that there wasn't too much celebrating going on, thinking of them back home. I wasn't in a big party mood myself.

'Another thing, mate,' he said, as he puffed at one of my duty frees, 'You've got to understand that with our young fellas being miles away, the only thing that stood between us and the yellow peril was the Yanks. If it hadn't been for that lot, we probably wouldn't be sitting here now. It's the Yanks who are the blue-eyed boys in Aussie right now!

We strolled down George Street. It reminded me of Oxford Street back home with its big stores. We compared Sydney's Hyde Park with the one in London. We stretched out on the grass on a warm, early autumn Sydney day, and the Aussie beer soon closed our eyes!

'Hi, mates,' said a chap as he stood over us. Let's 'ave your picture.'

'Of us?' we asked.

He flashed a card – the *Sydney*

'That'll please your old Mums!'

Sun, I believe it read. 'Over there under that tree.' We obliged. 'Let's 'ave your home addresses and

we'll send a copy back home for you. That'll please your old Mums!'

Later we boarded our liberty boat at Circular Quay that took us out to the ship in the bay. The Bosun handed us our station cards saying, ''ope you enjoyed your run ashore – you won't be seeing Sydney again for a while, cos we're off up to the islands tomorrow!'

Manus

'**B**ridge – radar.' 'Radar – bridge,' I answered. 'This is the navigator speaking. Your ranges and bearings that you pass to me want to be spot on during the next few days. I want to be the first RN ship to negotiate the Great Barrier Reef relying on radar alone! Don't let me down, will you?'

We didn't! Thirty hours later, 'Bridge – radar. Navigator speaking!' We didn't need telling as we had come to recognise his voice. 'Good show, radar!' he said.

Days before we had called in at Brisbane – well, not really Brisbane, but at some landing stage close by. We were at it again. Twenty-four hours later the hangar deck and flight deck were chock-a-block with Corsairs, Avengers and a sprinkling of Seafires. We didn't realise it, and I bet the Skipper was hopping mad, but the *Arbiter* was about to become part of the 'fleet train', a successful idea that the RN had adopted from the US Navy. It was a means of keeping the task forces at sea, supplying the ships with all the essentials, instead of the big boys returning to base too often. This role wouldn't suit a 'fighting man' like our Skipper!

As we went through the Coral Sea I thought of the old lad's words in the bar back in Sydney. It was here that the US Navy finally brought the Japanese to a halt and kept them out of Northern Australia. It was also here in the Coral Sea that the Pacific war finally turned in America's favour. It was here, and later at Midway, that the US Navy lost the fleet carriers *Lexington* and *Yorktown*. For their efforts the Japanese lost four fleet carriers and some cruisers. The lightning advances that the Japanese Army had made through the Pacific finally ground to a halt in the northern approaches to Australia.

We passed islands where the jungle came down to the water's edge, bearing such infamous names as Guam, Guadalcanal and other Solomon Islands, all back now in American hands. Close your eyes for a minute and you could see the US Marines storming ashore from their landing crafts!

The 'hook' went down in the sheltered lagoon of Manus, one of the Admiralty Islands, located off the north coast of New Guinea, a degree or so off the equator. It was the BPF's forward anchorage, and we were in imposing company. It seemed that without fuss the RN, now surplus to requirements in European waters, had left its Home Fleet bases in Pompey, Chatham, Devonport and Scapa Flow. We had left half the fleet in Trincomalee, up there in Ceylon, and now the other half was anchored here in this tiny spot in the Pacific Ocean. For company we had two battlewagons, four fleet carriers, five cruisers and a dozen or so DEs, which were now part of the United States Fast Carrier Force!

While I was leaning over the side and looking about me at our new surroundings with Charlie, a rusty old landing craft came alongside us.

'Hi there, you limey guys!' they yelled. 'We've got mail for you!'

Flicks on the flight deck

'Heavo, heavo, lash up and stow,' the pipe echoed around the anchorage, getting us all out of our bunks at 0530 hours. It was the first pipe of the day.

'Hands to fall in to clean ship,' followed by 'Hands to breakfast', followed again by 'Hands to clean ship'. That meant more scrubbing, hosing and washing down and general shipboard duties!

At 1300 hours came the pipe 'Hands to make and mend'.

This was the Navy's tropical routine when in harbour. Come midday, if you had an egg you could fry it up on the flight deck. Even when overcast, the day's heat was ever present!

Every so often when at the anchorage, come nightfall we had a film show, courtesy of the US Navy. The films and equipment were handed around the anchored ships.

'Duty watch to muster on the flight deck to erect screen for film show at 2000 hours.'

On duty or not, we all mucked in, manhandling benches up from the canteen flat. Of course, the two front rows were for the chairs, which we got from the wardroom! It was a popular pipe, along with 'Mail boat alongside' and of course 'Up spirits', when the older hands queued up for their tot. I was still a 'North Easter', or 'not entitled', as I was only 19 years old. However, in a few months' time I would come of age and be entitled to my first tot. If you declined, it meant an extra 6d a day in your pay book. As it was, some of the elders offered me 'sippers'. After that and the midday meal, there was nothing for it but to find, if you could, a shady spot and 'get your head down'.

Come 2000 hours, the 'cinema' was ready up on the flight deck. A 'Popeye' cartoon, a Western, a Bing Crosby or Gary Cooper film kept us up to date with the latest Hollywood epics! I looked about me. It reminded me of the old Greengate pictures down at Plaistow, though without the flitgun ladies and their sprays. Bouts of homesickness, prickly heat and dhobi rash were forgotten for two hours of magic!

The duty fo'c'sle watch had raised the anchor and, in company with two fleet tankers and other supply ships and a destroyer escort, we left the anchorage at Manus. I was off watch, meaning that it was my turn to sweep out and tidy up the mess and the adjoining 'heads'.

The leading hand of our mess stepped over the coaming. 'Kim,' he called, 'the divisional officer wants to see you in his cabin.'

'What for, 'ookey?' I asked.

'Dunno,' he replied. 'Smarten yourself up and get down there, and for goodness sake get into another pair of jeans. Those are falling off you.'

When in the Norfolk navy yard we had kitted ourselves out with US Navy 'slops', smashing blue jeans, to take the place of our regular Royal Navy overalls, T-shirts, white socks and soft slip-on shoes that were like carpet slippers to wear. As we scrubbed and scrubbed the jeans, like we did our collars, the blue dye came out and now my jeans, like everybody else's, were faded and threadbare. They were smashing to wear in the tropical heat, though!

I did as he suggested, rubbed my shoes up on the back of my legs, and popped into the 'heads' to get a few smudges off my cap. Satisfied, I went back into the mess.

'I've got just the man.'

'Don't forget to take your cap off when you go into his cabin,' I was told.

I knocked on the Divisional Officer's door.

'Come in.'

I stood in front of his desk remembering, just in time, to take my cap off, holding it nervously behind my back.

'Ah, O/S Kimberley, it's about time we made you up to Able Seaman. I see, looking through your papers, that you were one of the original crew that commissioned the ship in Vancouver. I see too that you will be 20 in September, and looking forward to drawing your tot, eh!'

I thanked him, still aware that I was nervously fiddling with my cap. I went to leave.

'Oh just one other thing while you're here. The Captain has asked me to find him a "runner" who must be a bright and reliable young man. I've got just the man, I told him. I'm sure you'll fit the bill down to a T.'

I opened my mouth but the words wouldn't come.

'Good, that's settled then. Report to the Captain's steward at 0800 hours tomorrow. Remember, from now on it's the rig of the day, with nice sharp creases in your shorts, eh! And don't forget this post relieves you of all your watch-keeping duties. Carry on A/B Kimberley,' he said.

Two days had passed since leaving Manus and we were now up here with the big boys. A destroyer was alongside, and I watched as the lads were pulling and heaving and wasting no time transferring over the supplies. Across the narrow strip of water the fleet carrier was getting her fill of oil from the fleet tanker. Similar scenes were being acted out all round.

Off-watch ratings as well as duty ones, radar, communications branch, cooks – one and all mucked in on these occasions. There were no dodgers, since we all realised the importance of the occasion – for them to get back north again and for us to get back south to another rendezvous! At a distance the destroyers kept a watch over the proceedings.

'Why me?' I asked myself as I realised that I was no longer to take part in the proceedings that were being enacted out below me. No more sea watches, no 'dogs', no shake for the middle watch that seemed never-ending, then, just as you did get your head down, 'Dawn Action Stations' being sounded. I was going to miss it all, especially my old jeans.

'Crikey!' I thought. 'Rig of the day at all times, shorts with those stiff white creases, and a spotless shirt, long black stockings, shoes that had to be polished every day. And that rotten old cap to be worn

at all times! They've always picked on me,' I thought, and remembered the time when old Mr Lethaby had handed me that badge at school.

'You'll make a fine school captain,' he had said. 'Wear the badge in your coat lapel at all times.'

I didn't really want to because,

like now, I felt that I wouldn't be one of the lads any more! I remembered once, when putting the key in the front door back at Khartoum Road, realising that the badge wasn't in my lapel.

'Crikey, I've lost it!'

Bob was as ever was doing his homework in the parlour. 'Where 'ave you been?' he asked.

'In the park 'aving a kick-about with Alf, Ernie, Eddy and a few others!'

'Well, let's go over there and see if we can find it,' he said.

'This is where we took our coats off for goal posts,' I said, and there was the badge lying on a clump of grass, the broken clip lying beside it!

'Mum'll soon get it fixed for you,' he said. Good old Mum, she fixed everything – she had it fixed at Hammets the jewellers in the Barking Road for a shilling!

As I stood outside the Captain's cabin at 0800 hours the next morning, the steward came out, looked me up and down, and said, 'You'll do.'

Captain's rounds

'ope he don't look in my locker!'

I quickly settled into the runner's routine. I took the signals from the Captain's cabin with a distribution list clipped on a board.

'You again,' the First Lieutenant would say as he signed the umpteenth signal that I had handed him that day! I then hurried off elsewhere to collect more signatures. I discovered parts of the ship that I never knew existed! Deep down in the engine room, Commander 'E' mopped his sweating forehead, tipped his stained cap further back on his head and signed. The navigator up on the bridge, along with the Officer of the Watch, did likewise.

It was a hot, sticky A/B Kimberley who, at the end of a long day, sat down on the deck in front of his locker and peeled off his not-so-white whites, his not-so-shiny

shoes and black stockings, and chucked his cap on top of his locker.

I had a wash down, then thankfully got into those faded worn-out jeans! Like a lot of the others, I forsook my bunk in the stifling hot mess deck and slung my hammock on the forward catwalk, spending the night, without any shakes for the middle watch, under the Pacific stars!

One day we waited outside his cabin, the Commander, 'Jimmy the One', the duty Petty Officer, and me at a discreet distance! The Captain was in a foul mood as he stepped out. It was no secret that he loathed the 'fleet train', with its dreary coming and going. Being who he was, he wanted to be up there with the big boys. Meeting up with them at pre-arranged latitudes

'Captain's compliments, sir...'

and longitudes wasn't his cup of tea at all!

The ship's company usually got the buzz that his rounds were under way, but not this morning. He caught us all with our trousers down!

Ours was the first mess he came to, and the first one he caught on the hop. There had been little time to sweep up or tidy up. He stepped over the coaming, and we all followed suit. What a sight for sore eyes it was – the mess was empty, the lads about their daily in-harbour routine.

'What a shambles, No 1!' he said, and after taking a deep breath, 'What a b—— mess!'

With that remark the duty PO put his hand over his mouth to stifle a laugh and the grin on his face.

'Er, yes, sir. I 'ave to agree with you. It's not dirty, though,' as he ran his fingers over the tops of the lockers and the ventilating shaft. 'Not a speck of dust anywhere, sir,' he added.

'I appreciate what you're saying, No 1. God help them if you had found it to be otherwise, but what a b—— mess it is,' as he eyed the full buckets of dhobying that lined the bulkheads, and the gear that was draped from anywhere but where it could be draped!

He stepped forward and opened an overburdened locker. As he wrenched open the door, its contents spilled out around his feet.

'Crikey,' I thought, ''ope he doesn't open mine!'

There was a knack to opening lockers. Do it too quickly, as he had done, and you spent the next ten minutes picking all the contents off the deck. Nice and easy does it, with one hand on the door and one over the shelves, and there was never a problem! He had obviously lost the knack when he had left the lower decks behind years ago.

'What's all this dhobying doing lying about the mess?' he demanded to know.

'Er, well, sir, it's the ship's laundry, it's US, sir.'

We were lucky that the *Arbiter* boasted a laundry. All American Navy ships had their laundries, and we, being American-built, had one too. However, months ago now it had broken down and had never been fixed.

Without waiting for a reply the Captain barked, 'Where's my runner? Get him to get the Commander "E" up here.'

I doubled away smartly, only too happy to get out of the stifling heat of the mess, which I am sure had shot up even more degrees these last few minutes!

I stood on the grating with Commander 'E' down in his engine room. 'With the Captain's compliments, sir.' I had got this patter off by heart now. 'Will you join him on the communications mess deck?' And I added 'Now.'

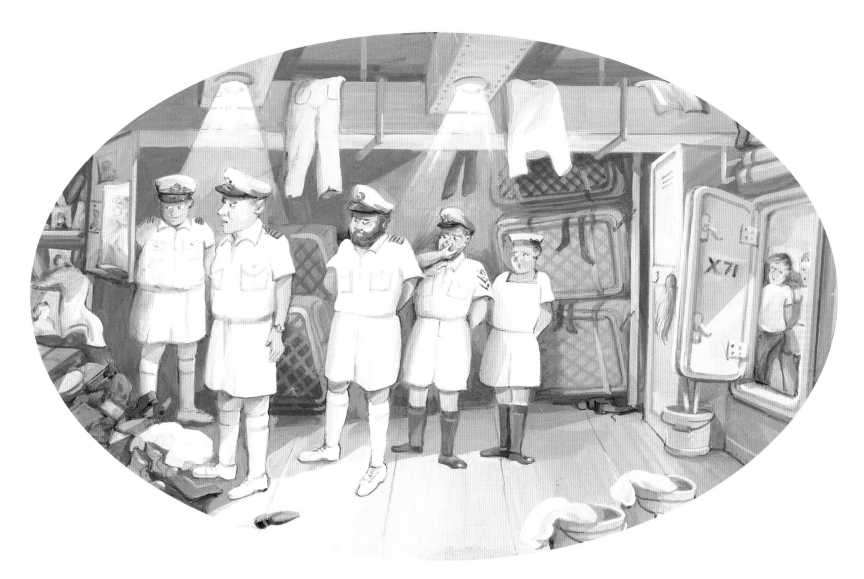

'What the hell does he want?'

Again hesitantly I said, 'He wants you to fix the ship's laundry, sir.'

'Fix the b—— laundry?'

He was 'wavy navy' and all that, and he could spell out a few home truths when he felt inclined! I had discovered this when asking him to sign yet another signal.

I stood aside as he stepped into our mess.

'Ah, Chief, sorry to drag you up here, but they tell me the ship's laundry is US. Can you fix it for us? Yes, I'm sure you can!'

'Aye aye, sir,' he replied and went back down below!

'What with these jeans and T-shirts, I sometimes wonder what navy we're in, No 1! And their hair, it's on their collars – haven't we a barber on board?.

Nobody dared tell the Captain that our barber, old 'Smithy', now had his feet under the table in a barber's shop in far-away Sydney, the barber's daughter being the attraction! He had scarpered when we were down there!

As we went into the next mess, the Captain turned and spoke to the 'Jimmy'.

'What we want is a good shake-up, No 1. I'll call for Sunday morning divisions – that'll be a start.'

'Crikey,' I thought. 'The last time I heard that mentioned was up in North Wales, when I dropped my rifle!'

Thankfully the skies opened on Sunday, and the flight deck was awash. Divisions was called off, much to everybody's relief!

'Another fine mess you've got us into, Stanley'

I had a grandstand view.

I used to take a quick glimpse at the signals as I took them round the ship. Curiosity at last getting the better of me, I made excuses to myself for doing so.

'Whatever I read, I'll keep it under my hat!' I thought.

One read: 'Unable to land all of my birds, holed in part of my flight deck, can you assist us?'

Two hours later, four of the big carrier's 'birds' were parked at the forward end of our flight deck. The forward lift well was packed with supplies of all sorts and, like our laundry of some weeks before, the lift was unserviceable, so we couldn't get them below into the hangar.

Most had come on well enough, helped or hindered by a PO who had never done the job in his life before, because when the squadron left us in India, the Fleet Air Arm flight deck crew had gone with them.

One, however, came in low. I was up on the bridge with my runner's duties, and had a grandstand view. He missed the arrester wire, and as we had witnessed so any times in our Atlantic days, he crashed full tilt into the parked kites. His mate, following up, witnessing it all, and zoomed away up and above us. The makeshift flight deck party were soon on the scene, dousing the flames and smoke that were licking around the plane's undercarriage.

Some wag on the catwalk called out to the stand-in flight deck PO, 'Another fine mess you've got us into, Stanley!'

Short of fuel, one Corsair ditched into the ''oggin'. We watched him go down with a splash, then a DE rushed up and fished out the pilot.

We watched him go down with a splash.

Mad dogs and Englishmen

'**M**ake and mend' had been piped.

'Who's for a run ashore?' 'ookey asked us.

We all laughed. The distant terrain looked as barren as Scapa Flow, though mind you it was a bit warmer!

He pointed to the nearest bit of rock and sandy beach, with its few palm trees bent over the water's edge. 'I'll ask permission from the Officers of the Day to let us take the whaler across there.' As an afterthought, he added, 'You can row, the lot of you?'

''course we can.' The idea was beginning to appeal to us.

The Captain had gone ashore to HQ in the forenoon, which left me free, so I would be able to join in with the others in the Bosun's party.

As I changed I realised that I was now able to join in with the rest of them, having a laugh and a joke. The sadness and misery that I had kept to myself for the last nine months was slowly leaving me, and was giving way to what I thought now must be the inevitable fact that Bob, along with thousands of others, would not be coming home...

'Pull together,' said 'ookey. We didn't make a bad job of it.

Our PO mechanic was sitting up with 'ookey.

'Coming for a run ashore?' we asked as we made our way down the ship's ladder to the whaler.

'Oh all right, I'll be the referee,' he said, noticing the football under somebody's arm! 'Football?' he added. 'You must be mad.'

In high spirits we pushed the whaler up the sandy beach. With a hefty blow Charlie kicked the ball, and like mad dogs and Englishmen we chased after it!

Half an hour later, after a swim, we lay about on the sand.

'Come on,' 'ookey said. 'We'd better be getting back on board.'

It wasn't until we were halfway back that he said, 'Where's old Durno, the PO? Silly old so and so – he's probably dozed off under one of those palm trees!'

We went back and looked for our popular Petty Officer. Let's face it, there weren't many places to look, but an hour later we gave it up. He'd vanished into the hot air!

Back on board our leading hand stepped forward and reported to the Officer of the Watch that PO Durno was missing. The Officer took down the details in his log, then called out the duty watch and they went off in the motor boat to try and find old Durno where we had failed. He suggested that the PO, while swimming with us, had become tangled with wrecked landing craft or other craft that lay about the beaches. Who knows if his cries for help had gone unheeded while we skylarked about in the water...

Later the motor boat came back without the Petty Officer. It was a sad bunch of blokes that sat down to our supper on the galley flat later that evening.

A job for old sawbones

The British Fleet's Task Force No 57, as it was known, was now operating close to the Japanese mainland. It was a formidable force, including the battlewagons *King George V* and *Howe*, together with four fleet carriers, half-a-dozen cruisers and a dozen or so destroyers. Meanwhile the 'fleet train' kept a respectable distance over the horizon while it continued to service and supply the big boys.

Our Navigator Officer, old 'Brains' as we nicknamed him, kept us up to date with events. The islands of Iwo Jima and Okinawa, Japan's last island outposts, had finally been taken by the US after bitter fighting. Our aircraft carriers *Formidable* and *Victorious* had been severely damaged by kamikaze suicide planes, but their armoured decks had saved them from complete disaster.

We had also heard on the grapevine that an American escort carrier like ours had suffered a similar attack. Fire had broken out and she had capsized and sunk. We trod our own wooden flight deck with some apprehension after that news!

Supplies were running low and as we returned to Manus. I glanced at the signal clipped to my board. 'Request to come alongside, seaman with suspected appendicitis requiring immediate medical attention. Weather is deteriorating, request to come alongside as soon as possible.'

The Pacific Ocean is not all deep-blue seas and blue skies – it can be as grey and angry as the Atlantic. It looked that way as the destroyer inched her way alongside us. The 'train' had disappeared over the horizon, and the big ship and the small ship were left to themselves to sort out this delicate operation!

Small ships, or the 'boats' – destroyers, frigates, sloops and the like – didn't look too kindly at their larger counterparts. The 'boats' thought that us bigger 'uns spent too much time swinging round the buoy in harbour, and had too many home comforts! Meanwhile, they were maids of all work, taking on board all the rough weather that made life one long, drenching experience!

Today, though, we were able to offer them a helping hand. It required all the skills of the seamen, officers and hands alike, on both ships, to bring this operation to a successful conclusion. The ships came together as one at a steady 8 knots or so, while the suspected appendicitis victim was eventually hauled across the narrow strip of water.

'Bunts' turned to me saying, 'Crikey, I'd sooner keep me appendix than let our old sawbones get his hands on me!'

On this occasion good-natured banter passed between the two watching crews as we parted company. The Officer of the Watch, with an audible sigh of relief, turned to 'Bunts'.

'Send a signal: "Do you want him back when we've finished with him?"'

'You can keep him,' came the reply. 'It'll be one less mouth for us to feed!'

Hong Kong

The signal read: 'A Superfortress of the US Army Airforce, on August 6th 1945, dropped the world's first atomic bomb on the Japanese city of Hiroshima.'

'So what?' I thought. 'Thousands of bombs have been dropped all over the place since 1939. What's so special about this one?'

I carried the message around to the various heads of departments. It was followed by a similar signal two days later. It was a different city this time though – Nagasaki.

The usual nattering and hubbub died away in the mess as the Captain's voice came from the speaker. Anything he had to say, we were all ears!

'This is the Captain speaking. I received at 1600 hours today a signal from Admiral Fraser at GHQ in Sydney.' A pause, then he went on. 'It is a signal of historic importance. It reads: "To all ships in the British Pacific Fleet. Yesterday, August 14th, the Japanese Government, with its military leaders, accepted the Allies' conditions and terms of complete surrender! A formal agreement will be signed on the US Navy's battleship *Missouri* September 2nd in Tokyo Bay, Japan."'

There was another pause. 'That is all,' he ended.

His announcement was greeted with complete silence for a minute or more. Then the cheering and back-slapping went on and on. Nobody could contain themselves. The flight deck, lit up now by the bridge searchlights, was packed in the early hours. Who could wish or hope to get any sleep on a night such as this?

The Captain came up on to the bridge with a loud hailer in his hand. 'For he's a jolly good fellow,' we all sang.

He held up his hand and quietened us. 'Another signal,' he said with a smile.

As with the previous one, I knew what was in it!

'I have instructions to proceed to Hong Kong as quickly as possible,' and with a wave to the lower deck he left the bridge.

We went alongside in Hong Kong and as we did so boats of all shapes and sizes clamoured around us. Within the hour we were lowering buckets of our spare food down to them. Whole families seemed to live on these tiny craft – grandparents, parents, sons and daughters all reached up for our buckets! Our old Chief Buffer stood looking down at the scene below.

'Oh, it's the usual cry, no different to when I was here in '37. It was still the same begging cries then!'

The 'Jimmy' came along and put a stop to it, saying, 'They'll be selling our gash food ashore before the night's out!'

They descended on us, this army of Chinese coolies. I had always thought that Chinese were little people, like they were in Vancouver, forever dashing about with their laundry baskets. These blokes were

'Oh crikey, come and 'ave a look at this!'

huge, with bulging muscles rippling under their threadbare clothing! They unloaded the ship of all of its supplies, which only a few weeks before had been destined for Task Force No 57. It wasn't long before we were offering them our duty frees and making them at home on the mess decks!

The First Lieutenant was furious when he discovered them wandering about the ship.

'Just because the war's over, discipline must be observed at all times.'

From then on sentries were posted all round the ship.

We couldn't believe it later, when we went ashore and discovered the remains of a cinder football pitch. On the puddles and weed-strewn ground there were clearly the remains of broken-down goal posts and the familiar white lines. It confirmed that this was a relic of

We soon got a game going between the messes.

the RN's long-ago association with Hong Kong! We soon got a game going between the messes and spent more time on our backsides than our feet!

Later, washing and getting the bits of cinder out of my hair, I heard Charlie bawl out, 'Oh crikey, come and 'ave a look at this. I ain't ever seen anything like this before.' Jokes and words failed him and us as we gazed at what he had found. He turned back the seams of his clean shorts and vest, where the bugs were lined up like soldiers on parade! We rushed off to inspect our own clothes. They were like Charlie's!

We vacated the ship for two whole days, and camped out in the dismal surroundings of broken-down warehouses! Few of the messes escaped. We laid out our belongings on the flight deck, then they and the whole ship was fumigated. We now realised what the 'Jimmy' had been going on about a week before, when he stormed, 'Don't encourage these people on to the mess decks!' An experienced Navy man of pre-war days, he knew what our coolie mates could bring on board with them!

For weeks the ship reeked of carbolic!

The Captain goes ashore

The Captain mustered us on the flight deck for the last time. 'It seems their Lordships at the Admiralty want me ashore. As from tomorrow I have a new job – I have been appointed Commodore of Hong Kong.'

There were cries of, 'Shame, don't leave us, Skipper!'

He held up his hand to silence us. 'The Commander will also be leaving. He is to take up a new appointment as Captain of a ship that is due here shortly. The First Lieutenant will, therefore, be in command of the *Arbiter* as from tomorrow.'

There were enthusiastic cheers at this piece of news, as the 'Jimmy' was a popular bloke.

'Now for the good news. The ship will be leaving in the next few days for Sydney.'

I had gathered this bit of information from my signal's board, though I never knew of the wondrous bit of news that was to follow.

'The ship will take on in Sydney much-needed supplies for the new garrison here in Hong Kong. On its return the *Arbiter* will sail for the UK!'

The silence was broken by cheers and more cheers, even louder and longer than those that greeted the news of a few weeks back! Caps were thrown high into the air, and all discipline was forgotten as cheer after cheer echoed around the anchorage in Hong Kong!

On my last day as the Captain's runner I was surprised when his steward asked me to step inside his cabin. I did so hesitantly.

'It's all right, Kim, he's down in the wardroom 'aving a farewell drink, I wouldn't wonder!'

There were suitcases and trunks packed and labelled, but one case remained open on a chair.

'Last one,' said the steward as he put some photo frames in it. 'That's the Skipper's missus,' he said. ' I've known them for years.'

He popped into the tiny galley saying, 'I've deserved a cuppa after packing up that lot.'

I was surprised when he handed me one. The cup and saucer were just like those out of Mum's best tea set back home!

'He won't be missing this old tub. Blooming "fleet train," he deserved better than that, what with all the decorations he's got up. He deserved better!'

We finished our tea. 'Give me a hand down with this lot, will you, lad?'

We two handled the trunks down to the hangar deck. From there two seamen, under the steward's watchful eye, took them down the gangway, where a 1930s-looking Humber saloon was waiting. I went back up to the cabin for the other two cases.

I stepped over the coaming and was taken aback when I saw the Captain saying his goodbyes to the First Lieutenant and the Officer of the Day. I could hardly push past him so I lowered the cases to the deck.

'Well, get the old thing back to the UK safe and sound, No 1,' I heard him say.

I stood there awkward-like, and as he went to brush past me, he stopped. 'Well,' he said, 'it's my runner, isn't it?'

I was astonished and tongue-tied when he spoke to me.

'Looking forward to the trip back home are you, lad? Hostilities-only rating are you? What were you up to before the war, then?'

'I was at school, sir,' I blurted out.

'School?' he said.

'That's right, but I was a ledger clerk for a bit before I joined up.'

'Pen-pusher, eh? Well, good luck to you, my boy.'

I was more astonished than ever when he held out his hand.

'Well, shake it then,' the Officer of the Day muttered out of the corner of his mouth.

The steward came up the gangway for the two cases. The RN driver opened the door of the big old Humber, the steward got in beside the driver, and our Captain, with a last salute to the ship, was off to his Commodore's job!

Under that bridge again

'Can I see you home?' I asked her. I was no dancer but she had helped me around the floor in the serviceman's club.

'It's not really allowed, but it won't hurt just this once,' she said.

Daphne, a bank clerk by day, came into the club twice a week, along with 20 or so other girls, to help us to forget our worries and the fact that we were thousands of miles away from home.

'I live in the suburbs – it means a train ride across the bridge.'

'That'll make a change,' I replied. 'I'm used to going under it!'

The view from the Sydney Harbour Bridge by night was more spectacular than sailing under it by day. We walked up the winding steep road dotted mostly with

'Well, Daphne, I've kept my part of the bargain.'

bungalows, with a few houses in between. It reminded me of back home. The bungalows, with their white-painted picket fences enclosing well-kept gardens, were just like suburban London, except for the fabulous view across the harbour! There were no street lamps, and a brilliant full moon lit up everything.

The seat we sat on, opposite her home, reminded me of the ones around the fountain in Balaam Street Park. 'That's my uncle's,' she said, as she pointed to the car parked in the driveway. 'He's come out for the day to see Mum.'

'Can I go and have a look at it?' I asked.

'Of course – but why?'

'Tell you in a minute,' I replied. It was, as I thought, a Hillman Minx saloon just like the one Bob had until the Blitz. 'Yes it is, it's a Minx, like my brother had before the war!'

'You have a brother then?' she asked. 'Any sisters?'

'No, just Bob and me!'

Looking at the old Minx in the driveway, it brought back for me a lot of happy memories of those carefree days before the war.

'I've a brother,' she said, 'but it all seems so long ago now.' She looked sad when she said, 'He went to North Africa, and then on to Italy and was reported missing.'

'We're both in the same boat, then.' And I told her of Bob.

'I just can't begin to tell Mum that after all this time we must now give up all hope of ever seeing him again!' she said.

I agreed with her, saying that I felt the same as she did.

'I'll have to tell her my true feelings soon,' she said.

Sitting on that old seat in the moonlight we made a pact. She was to tell her mother what she felt and tomorrow I would write and tell my own mother my feelings. And with a laugh we shook hands on the deal.

'Oh, there's Uncle,' she said. The front door opposite had opened. 'Come and meet Mum and Uncle.'

'I ought to be getting back on board,' I replied.

'Oh, don't worry! Uncle will drop you off at Circular Quay on his way back to town! This is Ken from England. This is my Mum and Uncle Fred.'

We shook hands and Uncle Fred gave me a good old Aussie slap on the back.

'Nice to meet you, mate. Can't

have this,' he added. 'Let's go back inside and have a beer, if that's all right with you, Mum,' he said to Daphne's mother.

I told them that this was now to be my last visit to Sydney and that we were off back to the UK after unloading in Hong Kong. They were pleased for me. We said our goodbyes at the front door of that cosy little home.

'Can I have your address?' I asked her. She handed me a folded slip of paper. 'I'll send you a Christmas card,' I said.

'With lots of your snow on it,' she replied.

'Lovely girl, is our Daphne!' said Uncle Fred on the way back to Sydney.

'She is,' I replied. 'I just wish she lived a bit nearer home!'

He laughed and dropped me off at Circular Quay. Twenty minutes later I reached into my locker, took out my pen and pad, went down to the canteen flat and joined a few others who were writing home. This time I found it easy to write about my feelings for Bob. It was, however, the hardest letter I had ever written in my young life! I sealed the envelope and popped it

in the ship's mail box, knowing that it would go ashore in the morning, before we went back up to Hong Kong.

I said to myself, 'Well, Daphne, I've kept my part of the bargain.'

She would, I know, keep hers!

I looked at the slip of paper she had handed me with her address. It read, 'Don't forget my Christmas card. Love, Daphne.'

Jumping crackers

They set about us in a market place.

The *Arbiter* was unloaded of its foodstuffs, clothing, bedding, medical supplies and the other necessities of life. This time round our coolie mates were restricted to the gangway and the hangar deck only – the 'Jimmy' wasn't going to allow the bug epidemic of some weeks before catch us out again!

We were granted shore leave into mainland China, and in doing so the First Lieutenant spelled out a few 'dos and don'ts' – in fact, all 'don'ts':

Don't eat anything ashore
Don't drink anything ashore
Don't go up any dark alleyways ashore
Don't go with any woman ashore. Remember that in a month or so you will be back with your loved ones
Don't let the Navy down, and above all don't let them down back home
Liberty men will fall in at 1600 hours
Dress of the day will be No 1s or optional No 5s.

We had only ever got into No 5s when practising 'abandon ship' drill back in Manus. Then we had jumped off the fo'c'sle or quarter deck while the whaler stood by below to heave us out of the water! When waterlogged No 5s weighed a ton, and after going down and down and coming up and up, I was just grateful to grab hold of the boat-hook that was offered me. I hung on to it for dear life, thinking that one day the boat-hook might not be available!

But that was all history now. I pulled the No 5s from underneath the palliasse on my bunk, admiring the 'seven seas' creases that I folded them into months before.

We boarded the Hong Kong-Kowloon Ferry with, it seemed, half the population of Hong Kong. The waterfront was a teeming mass of shanty-town dwellings that reached into the water, with small boats of every description riding along on the gentle swell. Amongst the shabbiness and the poverty of it all, there was excitement and happiness, with lanterns and flares illuminating the crowded thoroughfares and market places.

We jostled along with the crowds, and people were forever touching and pointing at us! Shop-keepers and stall-holders tempted us into their open-fronted emporiums. Elaborate ivory figurines, handsome carved trinkets, fans, lanterns and beautiful silk goods lay all around us.

'All vellee cheap for sailor boys!' was the cry.

I thought that it could be only a few months ago that they had been offering the same wares to the Japanese. To fill out my 'rabbit' case I bought a kimono and some silk scarves.

They must have followed us for a while and bided their time. It was now dark, and New York, Sydney or Vancouver just couldn't match up to the sheer exuberance we experienced in Kowloon, nor could those famous places match up to Kowloon's fireworks! They set about us in a market place with their 9-inch-long crackers. They had us leaping and dancing about for all our worth, and our immaculate No 5 bell-bottoms were scorched, singed and smoke-stained. Pigs and chickens scattered in all directions. We sought refuge in an emporium, where we felt obliged to buy more 'rabbits', the old Chinaman saying, 'It's our way of saying hello!'

Later the Officer of the Watch looked at us, saying 'What have you been up to?'

'Oh, it's an old Chinese custom of welcoming the RN to Kowloon,' we said.

'It's an old Chinese custom...'

Christmas carols

'We have two calls to make,' the First Lieutenant told us. 'The first will be Manila, then Singapore. We are to repatriate civilians held by the Japanese since Singapore fell. There will be about 60 in all, men, women and children.

'The women will be accommodated in the Officers' quarters, the children, at least the older ones, in the sick bay. The menfolk will be accommodated on the hangar deck. The canteen and galley flats along with the fo'c'sle will be out of bounds to all ratings during the afternoon and the dog watches.'

They came aboard in Manila and Singapore, and we helped them up the gangway with their small bundles of belongings. From out of the China Sea we turned north up the Malacca Straits and out into the Indian Ocean.

We skylarked about up on the flight deck and our passengers quickly lost their shyness. There was no Commander 'F' to give us a rollicking as the tennis ball went whizzing up and down the deck.

We stood with them on the fo'c'sle as we watched the dolphins play in the ship's bow wave. Sea mile after sea mile they accompanied us across the Indian Ocean, then, gone for hours at a time, they came back much to the children's delight. It seemed that they were putting on a special show for them, as they leapt out of the sea, their sleek bodies glistening in the sunlight! It also seemed as if they were forever pushing us nearer and nearer home!

Later the navigator stepped into the mess. I had had the previous middle watch, and was endeavouring to get a bit of shut-eye. But sleep these days was proving difficult, with all the excitement going on.

'Ah, you're the man who did those splendid crossing-the-line scrolls.'

'Er, that's right, sir,' I replied.

'I've another little job for you. Christmas Day is in ten days' time. I'm giving a little party for our guests, with carols and all that. The First Lieutenant has agreed to be our Father Christmas.'

He turned to the mess saying, 'I'm looking for some carol singers. How about it, lads?'

He got all the volunteers he wanted from our mess!

Turning back to me he said, 'I've found this Christmas carol book in the wardroom. Be a good man and copy, say, about 24 sheets of the most popular carols.'

He handed me a pen and a large writing pad. 'Oh, and here's a box of coloured pencils.'

I recognised these, as we often used them on the plots in the operations room.

'Perhaps you could head each sheet with some flowery lettering, and perhaps a sketch of the ship, what!'

Old 'Brains' soon had the ship's company scrounging bits of this and that to make simple small toys for his Children's Christmas Party!

On the day a small stage was set up on the forward lift, up on the flight deck, and a string of light bulbs and flags was hung about. The choir was in place, each member holding a piece of my sheet music.

The 'Jimmy' appeared, his flaming ginger beard disguised with cotton wool, as were the tops of his sea boots. The pièce de résistance was his duffel coat, the hood daubed with bright red lead paint! The choir sang and we all joined in. After each child was handed some small hand-crafted gift of sorts, an elderly chap, encouraged by his wife, climbed up on the dais, and thanked us for our efforts. The 'Jimmy' replied, saying that it was our privilege to escort them all safely home.

The party ended when we hoisted him shoulder-high and carried him around the flight deck! The sun sank down into the Indian Ocean and brought our Christmas Day 1945 to a close.

In the Suez Canal we spied a sparkling, nearly refitted cruiser! Of course we had to give the crew what for, remembering the way that we had been put through the mill some 12 months ago! We then passed through the Med and out into the Bay of Biscay, and with it came a change in the weather. Out came our black winter jerseys, and games up on the flight deck were abandoned as the old Atlantic rollers came charging at us!

At last the ship turned into the Firth of Clyde, and went alongside the jetty where months previously we had unloaded the last consignment of US planes. Two coaches were waiting for the civilians. They went ashore, huddled up in warm navy blankets, and they gave us a wave as they boarded the coaches. Two hours later the fo'c'sle party secured us to a buoy at the tail of the bank off Greenock.

At the tail of the bank

She had been my home for the last two years.

Coming up from Gibraltar, the 'Jimmy' had asked for volunteers to take the ship back to America. There was no shortage of these; it seemed that some of the lads couldn't resist one last stroll around New York! I wasn't a volunteer – I just wanted to stroll around my old home towns of Romford and Hornchurch!

As I lay up on my bunk that night I looked along the ventilation trunking, which was about 12 inches above my head. There I had religiously scratched with the front-door key that I kept on my key-chain 'New York', 'Detroit',

Bob's photo, taken in Canada, was on top of the wireless.

'Chicago', 'Vancouver' and all the other places that it had been my good fortune to see.

'I've been about a bit,' I thought. 'Crikey, how lucky too! How many sea miles – 100,000? 150,000? And here I am without a scratch to show for it! I have been so lucky. Other poor blokes had gone just 25 miles across the Channel and would never be coming home.'

I wondered how Alf Barrett and Ernie Bright, old Chas and my other Balaam Street mates had fared. Where were they now, I wondered? Would we ever get back to those kick-abouts in the park; those Saturday afternoons down at Upton Park, and queuing up outside the pictures on Sunday nights? With these thoughts buzzing around me, sleep was impossible.

We left the *Arbiter* just as the late-afternoon winter's sun went down over the distant hills above Helensburgh. Seagulls screeched around us and my home for the last two years, which had kept me warm and dry (too warm at times). We lost sight of her as we turned around the bow of the *Queen Mary*, on whose gangway we could see the US servicemen with their packs on their backs, like us going home. I remembered her as a speck on the horizon off the Isle of Wight.

'Is that really the *Queen Mary*, sir?' we had asked old Mr Solly. Years ago now it seemed.

I had also seen her in New York. They had their Empire State Building and everything else, but nothing like our 'Queens'! I had seen her, or so we thought – which one we didn't know – out there in mid Atlantic on the PPI radar screen. We were chugging along at a steady 12-14 knots, then almost off the screen, 20-25 miles distant, the green 'blip' came up.

'Fast-moving echo,' we had reported to the bridge, giving the bearing and range as well.

'Keep a watch on it, radar,' the Officer of the Watch had said. 'It's most likely one of the "Queens".'

There was no time to watch it, for as quickly as she came on the screen, at her maximum speed of 32 knots, she was gone! They said ashore in Greenock that they could put their clocks right when the 'Queens' left for New York and arrived back off the tail of the bank.

Early afternoon the next day I put my case down on the doorstep of No 8; I had left my kit bag and hammock in the left luggage office at Romford Station. 'That's all right, jack,' the man had said when I told him I would collect them in a day or two.

'Bump, bump, bump,' I heard as Paddy came down the stairs. Mum, in a letter, had said that he followed her 'all over the place'. She opened the door. The sadness

and anxiety that had lined her face 16 months ago was now thankfully replaced with a big smile. She stood there, our Mum of old.

'Ken,' she said, 'you're home!'
I put my case down on the lino in the hall, and she helped me off with my raincoat. I put my cap up on the hall stand.

'I'll make a pot of tea,' she said as we went in to the living room.
I looked across at the wireless that stood as ever in the corner on the small table, with its lace cloth

on it as it had always been! Bob's photo, taken in Canada, was on top of the wireless. Next to it, in a vase, was a bunch of early spring flowers.

'Home is the sailor, home from the sea'

I had been home a day or two when Mum handed me the letter from the Air Ministry. It was dated 8 August 1945.

'Madam,

I am directed to inform you with regret, that in view of the lapse of time and the absence of any further news of your son, Flight Sgt A. J. Kimberley, since he was reported missing, action has now been taken to presume for official purposes that he lost his life on 10 September 1944.

In conveying this information, I am to express to you the sympathy of the Air Ministry.

I am your obedient servant,
R. Randall
Director of Personnel Services

'You've had it all this time,' I said. 'Why didn't you let me know?'

'Silly,' she said. 'I didn't wish to upset you when you were all those thousands of miles away. I wonder what really happened to our Bob...'

I avoided answering her, as I reached for the teapot and poured another cup of tea.

'Never mind, Ken, you're back home now for good and that's all that matters,' she said with a smile.

Like all leaves, this one flashed past.

'Well, I'm only down at Chatham now,' I said. 'At the least I will be home once a week.'

'They won't be sending you away again, will they?' she asked.

''course not,' though behind my back I crossed my fingers!

I was given a red station card. 'Port watch again,' I thought.

'Nelson Block, Mess No 4,' I was told.

'Oh, one higher up this time.'

I had taken a dozen or so steps away from the gatehouse, kit bag over my shoulder, hammock under my arm, when a voice said, 'You there, what do you think you're up to?'

I took no notice and walked on.

''ere, mate,' the leading hand said. ''e's talking to you.'

'Me?' I asked, and turned round to face the voice.

The Sub-lieutenant came up to me. 'Don't you know what the rig of the day is?' he stormed.

'Well, er, sir, I've just come in.'

'Just come in or not, get that white cap off and your black one on. You're not out East now! You're in RNB Chatham!'

My looks must have conveyed my thoughts when he said, 'Right! Get your black cap out of your kit bag now!'

It was, I knew, deep down in my kit bag. I hadn't seen it for months! 'Crikey,' I thought. 'I bet it'll be all squashed up.' It was.

'That's more like it,' he said when I found it.

'Miserable old so and so,' I thought as I packed everything back in my kit bag. 'Don't he know the war's over?'

During the next five months I spent as much time at home as I did in the barracks. Spring and early summer came, and we all gave the drafting office as wide a berth as possible. Late summer arrived and with it came up my cherished 'demob' number.

'I'll have the chalk stripe, please, Miss, and the brown shoes!'

She handed me the suit and shoes, saying, 'This size will fit you a treat, jack. Oh, and what about a nice trilby?'

'No thanks,' I replied.

'Go on, take it, I'm sure it'll suit you!'

A few of us had a beer in the buffet at London Bridge Station and a last one for the road. Then I went down into the gents at Liverpool Street Station for a wash and brush up. Glancing in the mirror I decided the trilby wasn't for me. I took it off and left it by the hand basin.

I put the key in the front door and let myself in. Paddy lazily got off the fireside chair and came into the hall, tail wagging as ever. Making myself a cup of tea I sat down on the step by the back door in the warm, late-summer sunshine. Paddy ambled down the garden path and I followed him. No sooner than I had done so than I heard next door's kitchen door open.

'Kenny, Kenny!' came a cry. 'Footer, footer in the park!'

Mr and Mrs Hands had been firm friends to Mum during the war. They had a child with Down's Syndrome six or seven years old. We had become pals, and I often took him across to the local park, where we would kick a soft ball to each other. Little Johnny, his face always lit up with a great big warm smile, spent more time on his bottom, his little legs unable to support his podgy body. I leaned over the low fence, and as always lifted him as high as my arms would allow.

'Footer, Kenny, in the park!'

'That's right, old son, we've got all the time in the world now for you and your footer!'

Farewell bell-bottoms.

Paid off in my chalk stripe.

An 'Andrew' vocabulary, or a glossary of naval slang

I am indebted to Billy Wilkins, my cousin, who served in the Royal Navy during the war, for compiling this glossary. His memory proved better than mine!

Billy served on destroyers, a 'small ship' man. He joined HMS *Ashanti* in the Millwall Docks in London, and was a regular on the Murmansk run, the most hazardous of all convoy runs. The *Ashanti* was one of the last of four 'Tribal' class destroyers that survived the war from the original flotilla of 16 ships. 'Small ships' they may have been, but like the matelots who served in them they had big, strong hearts!

A/B	Able Seaman
Aft	Quarter deck
Amidships	Middle part of a ship
'Andrew', the	The Royal Navy
Battlewagons	Battleships, cruisers, etc
Bell-bottoms	Trousers widening towards the ankle
Boats, small ships	Destroyers, frigates, sloops, etc
'Buffer'	Bosun
'Bunts', Bunting tosser	Signalman
Buzz	Rumour
Captain of the Heads	Duty cleaner
Chief, Chiefy	Chief Petty Officer
Commander 'E'	Chief Engineer
Commander 'F'	Commander Flying (aircraft carriers only)
Dhobi	Washing
Heads	Wash place
Fo'c'sle	Forecastle, the forward part of a ship
Galley	Kitchen
'Guns'	Gunnery Officer

'Heavo, heavo, lash up and stow'	Morning call
Hook	Anchor
H/O	Hostilities-only rating
'Jimmy', No 1	First Lieutenant
Killick (or hookey)	Leading Seaman
Liberty Boat	Leave transport
Liberty men	Leave party
Make and mend	Free time
Matelot	Sailor, seaman
Mess deck	Living quarters
North Easter	Not entitled
O/D	Ordinary Seaman
'oggin	Sea
PO	Petty Officer
Pipe	Coxswain's whistle
Pusser	Anything supplied by the Admiralty
'Rabbits'	Presents
Seven seas	Creases in bell bottoms
Sippers (or tot)	Rum issue
Skipper	Captain
'Smoke', the	London
Sparks	Wireless operator

Stack	Funnel
'Subby'	Sub-Lieutenant
'Swain	Coxswain
Tiddly	Orderly looking, good
Tot (or sippers)	Rum issue
Two-ringer	Lieutenant
'Wavy navy'	Royal Navy Reserve
Wardroom	Officers' mess

Watches (normal)

Forenoon	0800-1200
Afternoon	1200-1600
First Dog	1600-1800
Second Dog	1800-2000
First Watch	2000-2400
Middle Watch*	2400-0400
Morning Watch*	0400-0800

*Dawn Action Stations

West Country Watches

Four hours off, four hours on
(Used when ship's complement is low)

HMS *Arbiter*

HMS Arbiter was a 'Ruler' class escort carrier, designed to provide air cover for convoys, and one of 26 such ships supplied to the Royal Navy by the United States Navy under the wartime Lend/Lease agreement. She was launched at Seattle as USS *St Simon* on 9 September 1943, and subsequently transferred to the RN in Vancouver. After the war she was returned to the USN on 3 March 1946, and in 1948 was converted to the merchant ship *Coracero*.

Displacement: 11,420 tons
Dimensions: 468.5ft (perpendicular length); 492.25ft (overall); 69.5ft (beam inside bulges); 25.5ft (mean draft at standard displacement)
Machinery: One-shaft geared turbine (built by Allis-Chalmers of Tacoma), SHP 9,350 = 17 knots
Armament: Two 4-inch anti-aircraft (AA) guns (two single mountings); 16 40mm AA (eight twin mountings); 20 20mm AA (20 single mountings); 24 aircraft
Hangar: Full-length under flight deck
Complement: 646

Festival Foods

Jenny Vaughan and
Penny Beauchamp

Heinemann
LIBRARY

www.heinemann.co.uk/library
Visit our website to find out more information about **Heinemann Library** books.

To order:
 Phone 44 (0) 1865 888066
Send a fax to 44 (0) 1865 314091
 Visit the Heinemann Bookshop at www.heinemann.co.uk/library to browse our catalogue and order online.

First published in Great Britain by Heinemann Library, Halley Court, Jordan Hill, Oxford OX2 8EJ, part of Harcourt Education.

Heinemann is a registered trademark of Harcourt Education Ltd.

Produced for Heinemann Library by Discovery Books Ltd.
Editorial: Helena Attlee, Geoff Barker, Nancy Dickmann and Tanvi Rai
Design: Jo Hinton-Malivoire and Rob Norridge
Illustrations: Nicholas Beresford-Davies
Cartographer: Stefan Chabluk
Picture Research: Laura Durman
Production: Séverine Ribierre

Originated by Dot Gradations Ltd.
Printed in China by WKT Company Limited

ISBN 0 431 11740 3
08 07 06 05 04
10 9 8 7 6 5 4 3 2 1

British Library Cataloguing in Publication Data
Vaughan, Jenny and Beauchamp, Penny
Festival Foods. – (A world of recipes)
641.5'67
A full catalogue record for this book is available from the British Library.

Acknowledgements
The Publishers would like to thank the following for permission to reproduce photographs: Patrick Ward/Corbis: p. **5**; Steve Lee: pp. **28**, **29**; all other photographs by Terry Benson.

Cover photographs reproduced with permission of Terry Benson.

Our thanks to Sian Davies, home economist.

Disclaimer
All the Internet addresses (URLs) given in this book were valid at the time of going to press. However, due to the dynamic nature of the Internet, some addresses may have changed, or sites may have ceased to exist since publication. While the author and publishers regret any inconvenience this may cause readers, no responsibility for any such changes can be accepted by either the author or the publishers.

Every effort has been made to contact copyright holders of any material reproduced in this book. Any omissions will be rectified in subsequent printings if notice is given to the publishers.

The paper used to print this book comes from sustainable resources.

Contents

Key

* easy

** medium

*** difficult

Words appearing in the text in bold, **like this**, are explained in the glossary.

Fstival recips

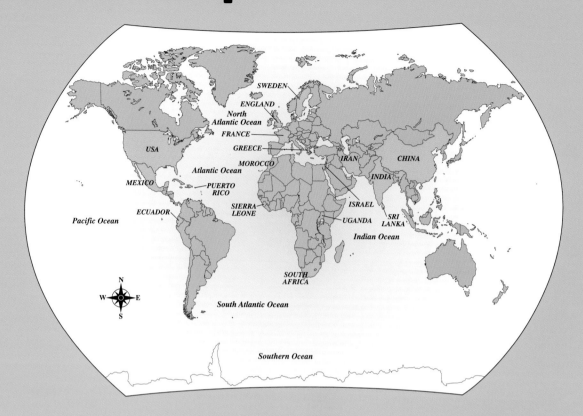

What is a festival?

A festival is a time when people celebrate to mark an important event. Whole families or groups of friends often eat together as part of the celebration. The food they eat will be something special – and usually there will be plenty of it.

Many of the special foods eaten at festivals are made using traditional recipes. The ones in this book are from the countries shown in yellow on the map above.

Festivals around the world

There are many different festivals celebrated all over the world. Some of the best-known festivals are linked to religions, such as Christmas and Easter for Christians.

Other festivals celebrate special days, such as New Year – but New Year may not always be 1 January.

For example, the Chinese New Year falls in early spring, while in the Hindu religion, New Year falls in October or November, and is celebrated at the festival of *Divali* (see page 42). (see page 42). The Jewish New Year – *Rosh Hashanah* – also falls at around this time of the year.

Some festivals belong to only one town or village. Others may be celebrated in slightly varied ways, but in many different places at the same time. Family occasions, such as weddings or birthdays, are also festivals of a kind. There are thousands of festivals all over the world, with an enormous variety of foods that are prepared especially for them.

Women carrying offerings of food during a festival in Bali, Indonesia.

Fasts

A fast is the opposite of a festival – a more solemn time, when people give up certain foods, or even all food, depending on their religion or custom. During Lent, many Christians do not eat meat or rich foods until the great celebration of Easter. Muslims keep to a fast that lasts throughout Ramadan – the ninth month of the Islamic year. At this time, Muslims may not eat or drink between sunrise and sunset. Ramadan ends with a festival called *Eid-ul-Fitr* during which special foods are eaten. Many fasting periods either begin or end with a special meal.

Ingredients

fresh thyme

chillies

fresh ginger

dried oregano

cinnamon

bay leaves

cumin

saffron

cardamom pods

Special foods

Festivals are special party times, and the food that goes with them is special, too. Festival recipes often include food that used to be too expensive for people to eat very often.

Spices

Spices used to be very expensive because in many parts of the world they had to be transported for hundreds of kilometres across the sea. They were only used to give food a unique taste on a really important occasion, such as a festival. Some spices, like cumin or cardamom, are sold as seeds or pods. They can also be ground up to make a powder. Cinnamon is sold in sticks made from the bark of a tree. All spices have quite a strong flavour, so you do not need to use very much of them.

Saffron

One of the most expensive spices is saffron. It is made from the orange-coloured **stigmas** inside a special kind of crocus flower. Luckily, you will only ever need it in tiny amounts. If you cannot get saffron, use a drop or two of yellow food colouring instead. This will not flavour the food, but it will give you the right yellow colour.

Ginger

Ginger is a spicy root that can be used in both sweet and savoury dishes. Some of the recipes in this book use fresh ginger. This is a root that must be **peeled** and either finely **chopped** or **grated** before it is used. Other recipes require ginger that has been dried and ground into a powder.

Chillies

A dish that contains chilli peppers will always taste hot. Chillies come in a variety of colours and sizes. Some are extremely hot while others have a much milder flavour. Always be very careful when you are handling chillies. Never rub your eyes or nose, as the chilli oil left on your fingers will make them sting.

Herbs

Herbs are used to add a delicious flavour to food. Thyme is a Mediterranean herb that thrives in hot, dry conditions. Like most other herbs, it can be used either fresh or dried. When herbs are dried it often makes their flavour stronger. Dried oregano is frequently **sprinkled** over pizzas in Italy. Bay leaves tend to be used to flavour soups and stews. In the past, people would only have used the herbs that they could pick near their homes, but today we can buy fresh or dried herbs from all over the world.

Before you start

Kitchen rules

There are a few basic rules you should always follow when you are cooking.

- Ask an adult if you can use the kitchen.
- Some cooking processes, especially **frying**, and those using **boiling** water or syrup, can be dangerous. When you see this sign, always ask an adult to help you.
- Wipe down any work surfaces before you start cooking, and then wash your hands.
- Wear an apron to protect your clothes, and tie back long hair.
- Be very careful when using sharp knives.
- Never leave pan handles sticking out, because you might knock the pan over.
- Always wear oven gloves to lift things in and out of the oven.
- Wash fruit and vegetables before you use them.

How long will it take?

Some of the recipes in this book are very quick and easy to make, while others are more difficult and may take much longer. The strip across the top of the right-hand page of each recipe tells you how long it will take to make each dish. It also shows you how difficult the dish is to make: every recipe is either * (easy), ** (medium) or *** (quite difficult). Why not start with the easier recipes?

Quantities and measurements

You can see how many people each recipe will serve by looking at the strip across the top of the right-hand page. You can multiply the quantities if you are cooking for more people. Avoid changing the quantities of ingredients in a cake or a loaf, as this will alter the time that it takes to **bake**.

Ingredients in recipes can be measured in two different ways. Metric measurements use grams, litres and millilitres. Imperial measurements use ounces and fluid ounces. This book uses metric measurements. If you want to convert them into imperial measurements, use the chart on page 44.

In the recipes, you will see the following abbreviations:

tbsp = tablespoon　　　g = grams　　　　　kg = kilograms
tsp = teaspoon　　　　　ml = millilitres　　　cm = centimetres

Utensils

To cook the recipes in this book you will need these utensils (as well as essentials, such as spoons, plates and bowls):

- baking foil
- baking tray
- **baking parchment**
- cake rack
- **chopping** board
- **colander**
- **draining** spoon
- large dried beans
- **fish slice**
- food processor or blender
- frying pan (with a lid)
- **grater**
- measuring jug
- round flan tin (20cm, non-stick)
- omelette pan (non-stick)
- **ovenproof** dish about 16 x 23cm
- pastry brush
- rolling pin and a pastry board
- 2-litre saucepan
- smaller non-stick saucepans
- set of scales
- sieve
- square and round cake tins (20cm, non-stick)
- sharp knife
- **whisk**

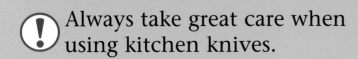

Always take great care when using kitchen knives.

Savoury dumplings (China)

Dumplings are often served during the festivities that mark the Chinese New Year. Nobody does any work during the festival, and so food is prepared in advance to be eaten later.

What you need

1 spring onion
fresh ginger root,
   about 1cm long
300g *pak choi*, or
   Chinese leaves
250g minced pork
1 tbsp soy sauce
175g plain flour

What you do

1 Wash the spring onion, cut off the root and **chop** finely.

(!) 2 **Peel** and chop the ginger root very finely.

3 Chop the *pak choi* or Chinese leaves very finely.

(!) 4 Bring a pan of water to the **boil**. Add the *pak choi* and boil for 3 minutes. **Drain** the leaves through a sieve, **rinse** them under a cold tap and spread them out on kitchen paper.

5 Thoroughly mix the **minced** pork, spring onion and *pak choi*, ginger and **soy sauce** together. Wash your hands.

6 Put the flour in a bowl and make a **well** in the middle. Gradually add 115ml water, stirring all the time with a fork to make a sticky **dough**.

7 **Knead** the dough on a floured board for 5–10 minutes, until it is smooth and stretchy. Roll it into a sausage shape with your hands.

8 Cut the dough into 16 equal pieces and then roll out each one to make a thin circle. Place a teaspoonful of filling on each circle.

9 Fold each circle in half, pressing the sides firmly together and then use a fork to seal the edges.

(!) **10** Bring a large pan of water to the boil. Drop 2 or 3 dumplings into it and cook them for 20 minutes. Take them out with a draining spoon.

11 Cook the rest of the dumplings in batches of 2 or 3. If you put too many in the pan they will begin to stick together. Serve with soy sauce.

Pescado n escabech (Puerto Rico)

Puerto Rico is an island in the Caribbean which lies between the continents of North and South America. This recipe is made during the Christian Holy Week – the week before Easter.

What you need

400g cod, haddock or hake, with bones removed
30g flour
¼ tsp paprika
60ml olive oil
¼ mild onion
small garlic clove
6 peppercorns
1 large bay leaf
salt and pepper
30ml white wine vinegar

What you do

1 Cut the fish into 4 pieces.

2 Place the fish pieces on a plate and **sift** the flour on to them. Make sure they are all covered with flour.

3 **Sprinkle** the fish with paprika.

(!) **4** Heat 2 tbsp of olive oil in a **frying** pan and fry the fish in it, piece by piece, for 4 minutes on each side. Don't cook the fish too much, or it will start to fall apart when you lift it from the pan. Use a **fish slice** to remove the fish from the pan.

5 Allow the fish to dry on kitchen paper.

(!) 6 Slice the onion and garlic thinly.

7 Put the fish pieces in the bottom of a shallow dish that measures about 16 x 23cm. Scatter the onion, garlic and peppercorns on top. Break the bay leaf into 2 or 3 pieces and place them among the fish.

8 Sprinkle salt and pepper over the fish and vegetables.

9 Whisk the rest of the oil with the vinegar and pour it over the fish. Cover the dish and keep it in the fridge until you are ready to serve it, **basting** the fish from time to time with the oil and vinegar. This dish is delicious served with cold rice salad.

Ramadan soup (Morocco)

This dish, which is called *harira* in Morocco, is a cross between a soup and a stew. It is made during Ramadan, a fast that lasts for the whole of the ninth month of the Muslim year. Muslims do not eat or drink between sunrise and sunset during Ramadan, and *harira* makes a nourishing meal that is especially welcome at the end of a day of fasting.

What you need

200g lean lamb
1 onion
115g tinned chickpeas, **drained**
2 tbsp olive oil
400g tinned, chopped tomatoes, including their juice
115g dried red lentils
60g long-grain rice
1 tbsp tomato purée
¼ red pepper, chopped
juice of 1 lemon
1 tbsp chopped fresh coriander, or fresh coriander and parsley mixed

What you do

1 **Chop** the lamb into pieces of 2 x 2cm or less.

2 **Peel** and **slice** the onion.

3 **Rinse** the chickpeas.

4 Heat the oil in a large pan and **fry** the lamb for about 5 minutes, until it is lightly browned on all sides.

5 Add the onion and cook gently. When it is soft, add all the other ingredients except the fresh herbs.

6 Add 1 litre of water and bring the soup to the **boil**. **Simmer** for about 30 minutes, until the rice and lentils are cooked through.

7 Add the coriander, or the fresh herb mixture, and simmer for another 5 minutes. Serve hot.

New Year omelette (Iran)

This omelette recipe is from ancient Persia, the country that is now called Iran. It is made for a New Year festival that dates back to the time before Iran became an Islamic country, over 1000 years ago. Persian omelettes are unusual because, unlike the French omelettes that we are all used to, they are frequently **baked** in the oven, instead of being **fried** in a pan.

What you need

2 spring onions
1 leek
40g fresh spinach
   leaves
1 sprig parsley
1 tbsp fresh oregano
   and fresh thyme,
   mixed
6 large eggs
salt and black pepper
25g butter

What you do

1 **Preheat** the oven to 170°C/325°F/gas mark 3.

2 Wash all the vegetables and dry them on kitchen paper.

3 Remove any damaged outer leaves from the spring onions and leek. Cut off the root and green shoots.

4 **Chop** the spring onions, leek, spinach and herbs very finely.

5 **Beat** the eggs in a large bowl.

6 Mix in the vegetables. **Season** with salt and pepper.

7 **Grease** an **ovenproof** dish with butter. The exact size of the dish is not important, but it should be about 20cm across. A round, non-stick cake tin is ideal.

8 Pour the egg mixture into the dish and cover it with foil.

9 Bake for 30 minutes, and then remove the foil. Cook for another 10 minutes, until the egg has set and the mixture is brown on top.

Fanesca (Ecuador)

This soup is eaten during Lent in the South American country of Ecuador, where many people are Roman Catholics. Many Catholics do not eat meat during Lent, and so this fish recipe is very popular. Dried salt cod – called *bacalao* – is traditionally used in this dish. It can be hard to find, so we suggest using fresh cod or haddock in this extra tasty version.

What you need

1 onion
1 garlic clove
25g butter
1 tsp dried oregano
1 tsp ground cumin
salt and freshly ground
    black pepper
100g long-grain rice
250g mixed, frozen
    broad beans,
    sweetcorn, runner
    beans and peas
500ml vegetable stock
2 level tbsp cornflour
350ml milk
175g skinless cod or
    haddock fillet

What you do

1 **Peel** the onion and **slice** it finely.

2 Peel the garlic clove and **chop** it finely.

(!) 3 **Melt** the butter in a large saucepan and **fry** the onion and garlic over a low heat until the onion is soft, but not brown. This will take about 5 minutes.

(!) 4 Add the oregano, cumin, salt, pepper, rice, frozen vegetables and stock. Bring to the **boil**. Reduce the heat and **simmer** gently for about 30 minutes.

5 In a small jug or cup, blend the cornflour with 4 tbsp milk. Then add the remaining milk.

6 Cut the cod or haddock fillet into chunks and add them to the saucepan. Cook gently for about 4 minutes.

7 Stir the cornflour mixture to make sure that it is smooth, then add it to the saucepan, stirring all the time. Cook, stirring, for about 3 minutes, until the mixture thickens.

8 Ladle the soup into bowls and serve at once.

ADDED EXTRAS

In Ecuador, the soup is served with chopped, hard-boiled eggs, **grated** cheese, chopped peanuts and chopped parsley on top – so you can do this too, if you like.

Jolloff rice (Sierra Leone)

This popular party dish is cooked throughout West Africa. It is often served at the festive meal following a wedding, or on other important, family occasions such as birthday parties. People adapt the recipe according to the number of guests they are entertaining. Add more rice to make the food go further.

What you need

1 large onion
1 red chilli (not too hot)
100ml groundnut oil
   (or palm oil if you
   can get it)
500g chicken pieces,
   stewing beef or lamb
2 tbsp tomato purée
1 tsp fresh thyme or a
   large pinch of dried
   thyme
salt and pepper
100g long-grain rice

What you do

1 **Peel** and **slice** the onion finely.

(!) 2 Cut the chilli in half lengthways, remove the seeds and then **chop** it. Always wash your hands after you have handled chillies. Never touch your eyes when handling chillies.

(!) 3 Heat the oil in a saucepan. Add a little of the chicken or meat and **fry** it for a few minutes, until brown on all sides.

4 Take the meat out of the pan, put it into a warm dish, and fry the rest of the meat, in batches, until it is all browned. It does not have to be cooked right through. Set aside and keep warm.

(!) **5** Put the onion and chilli into the pan that you used for the meat. Fry over a low heat for about 10 minutes.

(!) **6** Add the tomato **purée**, thyme, salt and pepper, and about 100ml of water. Allow the mixture to **boil**.

7 Return the meat to the pan and **simmer** for about 20 minutes, or until the meat is **tender**. You may need to add a bit more water from time to time.

8 Add the rice and 200ml of water to the stew. Let it simmer for about 15 minutes, stirring all the time. Add a little more water if it seems to be drying out. Once the rice is cooked, the dish is ready to serve.

Makaronada (Greece)

This is a Greek version of macaroni cheese. Like Roman Catholics, members of the Greek Orthodox Church often avoid meat during the fast of Lent – the time when Christians remember the story of how Jesus spent 40 days fasting in the wilderness.

What you need

300ml milk
50g butter
100g plain white flour
3 eggs
125g macaroni
salt and pepper
125g Cheddar cheese

What you do

(!) **1** Warm the milk, but do not let it **boil**.

(!) **2** **Melt** the butter in another saucepan.

3 Add the flour to the melted butter a little at a time, stirring all the time. Keep the heat under the saucepan low.

4 Add the milk to the flour and butter mixture, a little at a time. Keep stirring so that there are no lumps. When the sauce is thick and creamy, let it cool.

5 Break 2 of the eggs into a bowl. Using a spoon, lift out the yolks. Mix them into the sauce, along with the other, whole egg. You do not need the spare egg whites in this recipe.

6 **Preheat** the oven to 220°C/425°F/gas mark 7.

(!) **7** Bring a large pan of water to the boil, add the macaroni and cook it until it is soft. This will take about 10 minutes.

8 Carefully **drain** the macaroni and add it to the sauce. **Season** with salt and pepper.

9 Put half the macaroni and sauce in an ovenproof dish of about 16 x 23cm.

10 **Grate** the cheese. Spread half of the grated cheese over the macaroni. Spoon the rest of the macaroni and sauce over it and then **sprinkle** the top with the remaining cheese.

11 **Bake** for about 20 minutes, until the surface of the makaronada is golden.

WHITE SAUCE

The flour-and-milk sauce is usually known by its French name, which is béchamel sauce. If lumps form (they often do), push the sauce through a sieve, whizz it in a blender, or **whisk** it with an electric whisk. Do this before adding the eggs. If the sauce is too thick, just add more milk.

23

Peanut sauce for chicken (Uganda)

This sauce is eaten with roast chicken on special occasions, such as birthday parties, wedding banquets or other family celebrations. The recipe makes enough sauce for a 1.5kg chicken. In Africa it is often made with freshly roasted and ground peanuts. Always check that none of your guests are allergic to nuts.

What you need

1 large onion
2 tbsp vegetable oil
227g tin chopped tomatoes (with their juice)
4 tbsp crunchy peanut butter
240ml milk
salt and pepper
1.5kg roast chicken, sliced

What you do

1 **Peel** and **chop** the onion finely.

2 Heat the oil in a large saucepan and **fry** the onion until it is golden.

3 Add the tomatoes, peanut butter, milk and a pinch of salt and pepper. Stir everything together.

4 Cover with a lid and **simmer** for about 20 minutes.

5 Check the sauce regularly, and stir it to make sure that it doesn't burn. Add a little water if the sauce seems to be getting too dry.

6 Serve the warm sauce with **slices** of roast chicken.

Mancha manteles (Mexico)

Mancha manteles is a Mexican dish and its name means 'table-cloth stainer' – you will see why when you try serving it! It is made in midsummer, when Christians remember the importance of the Holy Communion or Mass during the Festival of Corpus Christi.

What you need

400g lean pork fillets
2 tbsp vegetable oil
400g chicken pieces
4 mild chillies
½ red pepper
30g flaked almonds
1 tbsp sesame seeds
1 tbsp white wine
  vinegar
200g tinned tomatoes
1 cinnamon stick
2 eating apples
1 unripe or nearly ripe
  banana
140g **drained** tinned,
  unsweetened pineapple

What you do

1 Cut the pork into 4 pieces.

(!) **2** Heat 200ml water in a pan, and then add the pork and let it cook gently.

(!) **3** Meanwhile, heat the oil in a **frying** pan and fry the chicken until it is brown on all sides, but not cooked through.

4 Add the chicken to the saucepan with the pork. Keep the oil in the frying pan as you will use it again later.

(!) **5** Cut the chillies in half lengthways, remove the seeds and then **chop** them finely. Always wash your hands after you have handled chillies. Never touch your eyes when handling chillies.

6 Remove the seeds from the pepper and chop it into small pieces.

7 Put the almonds, sesame seeds, chillies and red pepper in the frying pan and fry them, stirring all the time, until the almonds are just turning brown.

8 Add the vinegar and tomatoes to the frying pan. Cook for another 3 minutes before putting the red pepper mixture into the saucepan with the chicken and pork.

9 Add the cinnamon stick, and enough water to almost cover the mixture.

⊘ 10 **Peel** and chop the apples and banana, removing the apple core. Fry the fruit in oil for a few minutes and then add the pineapple.

11 Put the cooked fruit in the pan with the chicken and pork. Cover with a lid and **simmer** for 30 minutes. Remove the cinnamon stick before serving.

Pumpkin pie (USA)

Americans make this sweet, spiced pie to celebrate Thanksgiving. This festival dates back to 1621, when the early settlers in New England brought in the first harvest in their new country.

What you need

1 tbsp plain flour
300g ready-made **shortcrust** pastry
1kg fresh pumpkin
80ml milk
3 eggs
125g caster sugar
½ tsp ground nutmeg
½ tsp ground ginger
½ tsp ground cinnamon

What you do

1 Preheat the oven to 190°C/375°F/gas mark 5.

2 Sprinkle flour over a clean work surface. Roll out the pastry until you have a circle about 30cm wide.

3 Use the pastry to line a 20cm, round flan tin. Prick the base of the pastry case with a fork.

4 Put a 30cm square of **baking parchment** into the pastry case. Fill it with any large, dried beans. This will stop the pastry from puffing up in the oven.

(!) 5 Put the tin in the oven and **bake** the pastry for about 15 minutes. Then remove the beans and paper.

6 Cut the pumpkin into segments, remove the peel and seeds, **chop** and **rinse** 500g of the flesh.

(!) 7 Place the prepared pumpkin in a covered **colander** over a pan of **boiling** water and **steam** it for about 20 minutes, until it is very soft.

8 Put the pumpkin in a bowl with the milk and mash it. Let it **cool**.

9 **Whisk** the eggs, sugar, nutmeg, ginger and cinnamon together, and mix them into the pumpkin.

(!) **10** Spread the pumpkin mixture into the flan case. Bake it for about 40 minutes, or until filling has set. Serve hot or cold with whipped cream or vanilla ice-cream.

TINNED PUMPKIN

You can use a 500g tin of pumpkin instead of fresh pumpkin in this recipe. If you do use tinned pumpkin, you can leave out steps 6–8 in the recipe.

Tamil rice harvest pudding (Sri Lanka)

This dish is made by the Tamil people of Sri Lanka, to celebrate the rice harvest. Traditionally, it is made only from the purest white rice and fresh milk, as the pudding is an offering to the gods. It is cooked in a special pot, early in the morning, so that the first rays of the sun will strike the milk as it begins to boil.

What you need

600ml full cream milk
125g long-grain rice
1 short stick of
   cinnamon
pinch of crushed
   cardamom seeds
1 ripe banana
handful of raisins, dates
   or sultanas (or a
   mixture of all 3 fruits)
60g soft brown sugar

What you do

1 Put the milk in a non-stick saucepan.

(!) 2 Add the rice, cinnamon and cardamom and place it over a low heat. Bring it to the **boil**.

3 Let the rice **simmer** for an hour. Stir gently so that no rice grains stick to the bottom of the pan and burn.

4 When the rice has **absorbed** all the milk, check to see that it is cooked. Do this by testing 1 or 2 grains to see if they are soft all the way through. If the rice is not ready, add a little more milk and simmer for a little longer.

5 **Peel** and **slice** the banana. Add it to the rice, with the dried fruit and the sugar and stir well.

6 Leave the pudding off the heat for about 20 minutes, stirring it every now and again to stop a skin forming on top. This delicious pudding can be eaten hot or cold.

Crêpes (France)

The Christian fast of Lent starts on a Wednesday. The day before is called Shrove Tuesday. Traditionally, people used up all the rich foods in their larders on Shrove Tuesday, before the Lenten fast began the next day. This is why Shrove Tuesday is called *Mardi Gras*, (or fat Tuesday), in France. Pancakes, or *crêpes*, were a convenient way of using up eggs and milk or cream.

What you need

250g plain flour
pinch of salt
2 eggs
60g butter
500ml milk

What you do

1 In a mixing bowl, mix the flour and salt together.

2 Break the eggs into another bowl and **beat** them well.

(!) 3 **Melt** the butter in a **frying** pan.

4 Make a **well** in the flour and tip the beaten eggs into it.

5 Add the milk and about two-thirds of the melted butter. Leave the rest of the fat for frying the crêpes.

6 Beat all the mixture together to make a smooth **batter**. Let this stand for about an hour.

7 Add a little of the remaining melted butter to the base of a non-stick omelette pan and then place the pan over a gentle heat.

(!) 8 When the butter starts to smoke, add a spoonful of crêpe mixture to the pan. Tip the pan from side to side, so that as much of the base as possible is covered by the mixture. Cook for about a minute, until the crêpe bubbles, and then use a non-stick **fish slice** to flip the crêpe over and cook the other side.

9 Slide the crêpe on to a warm plate and cover it with greaseproof paper while you make the rest of the crêpes, one at a time.

TASTY FILLINGS

For a savoury meal, make a filling for your crêpe using mushrooms, cheese or ham. For sweet pancakes, try fresh lemon juice and sugar, or jam and cream.

Santa Lucia cakes (Sweden)

Swedish girls serve these special cakes on Santa Lucia's day, 13 December. Saint Lucia was an early Christian. Many of her fellow Christians went into hiding because the Romans wanted to punish them for their faith. She bravely took food to them.

What you need

75g butter
2 pinches of saffron
300ml milk, plus 3 tbsp
700g strong bread flour
7g dried 'easy-blend' yeast (usually, this means 1 sachet)
115g granulated sugar
pinch of salt
2 beaten eggs
handful of raisins

What you do

1 **Melt** the butter gently in a small pan.

2 Put the saffron in 300ml of milk in another pan and warm it until it is **tepid**.

3 Mix the flour, **yeast**, sugar and salt in a warm bowl, and make a **well** in the centre.

4 Pour in the warm milk and saffron, the melted butter and 1 **beaten** egg into the well and stir.

5 **Knead** the **dough** on a floured board for about 10 minutes. Add more flour to the mixture if the dough becomes too sticky.

6 Put the dough in a warm place and cover it with cling-film. Leave for about 90 minutes to rise (grow) to twice its original size.

7 Add the raisins and knead the dough again. Divide into 24 evenly-sized pieces. Roll each into a sausage shape.

8 Cover a baking tray with **baking parchment**. Put the shapes on this, curling them to make 'S' or 'C' shapes. Leave them to rise for another 30 minutes.

9 **Preheat** the oven to 220°C/425°F/gas mark 7. Make a **glaze** by mixing 3 tbsp of milk with the other beaten egg. Let it stand for 5 minutes, then brush it over the buns.

(!) 10 **Bake** the buns for around 10 minutes, until they are golden brown. **Cool** them on a cake rack.

Parkin (England)

This ginger cake is eaten in England at Bonfire Night parties on 5 November. The celebration reminds people about Guy Fawkes, a man who took part in a plot to blow up King James I and the Houses of Parliament on 5 November 1605. He was caught, but people have always remembered the story by building bonfires and letting off fireworks.

What you need

50g butter
150g golden syrup
100g treacle
200g plain flour
250g medium oatmeal
50g granulated sugar
2 tsp ground ginger
1 egg, **beaten**
1 tsp bicarbonate of soda
2 tbsp milk

What you do

1 **Preheat** the oven to 170°C/325°F/gas mark 3.

2 **Grease** a non-stick, square cake tin, around 20 x 20cm with a little butter.

(!) 3 Gently, **melt** the butter, golden syrup and treacle together in a large saucepan, until they are runny. Allow the mixture to **cool** a little.

4 Stir in the flour, oatmeal, sugar, ginger and egg.

5 Mix the bicarbonate of soda and milk, and add them to the mixture.

(!) 6 Pour the mixture into the cake tin and **bake** it for about 50 minutes.

7 Turn the oven off, keep the door closed, and leave for a further 35 minutes. The parkin will sink a little in the middle of the tin.

8 Cut the parkin into equal squares as soon as it is cool enough to eat.

Cape Malay milk tart (South Africa)

This recipe is Malayan in origin, but it is made by Malay families who live in South Africa. There it is a traditional dish served at family weddings. The tart can be eaten either warm or cold, whichever you prefer.

What you need

1 tbsp plain flour
300g ready-made **shortcrust** pastry
500ml milk
1 tsp vanilla extract
50g plain flour
pinch of ground cinnamon (optional)
2 eggs
60g sugar

What you do

1 **Preheat** the oven to 170°C/325°F/gas mark 3.

2 **Sprinkle** 1 tbsp plain flour on a work surface and roll out the pastry to make a circle about 35cm across.

3 Use the pastry to line a non-stick flan dish of about 20cm in diameter. Trim off the extra pastry and prick the base of the pastry case with a fork.

4 Put a 30cm square of **baking parchment** into the pastry case. Fill it with any large, dried beans. This will stop the pastry from puffing up in the oven.

5 Put the tin in the oven and **bake** the pastry for about 15 minutes. Remove the beans and paper.

6 Warm the milk in a non-stick pan and add the vanilla **extract**.

7 In another non-stick pan, mix the flour with a little of the milk and vanilla mixture, stirring all the time, until you have a smooth **paste**.

8 Gently heat this paste, adding the warm milk a little at a time and stirring it so that no lumps form. When all the milk has been added, add the cinnamon if you are using it.

9 Let the sauce **simmer**, stirring until it thickens. This should take about 5 minutes. Let it **cool**.

10 **Beat** the eggs with the sugar, and gradually add them to the milk sauce mixture, stirring all the time.

11 Pour the milk sauce mixture into the pastry case and bake for about 25 minutes.

Honey cake (Israel)

This honey cake is made for *Rosh Hashanah*, a festival that falls in autumn and marks the beginning of the Jewish New Year. It is traditional to eat certain foods at this time, and this is one of them.

What you need

200g plain flour
pinch of salt
1½ tsp baking powder
1 tsp mixed spice
50g granulated sugar
4 eggs
250ml runny honey
75ml vegetable oil
1 tsp instant coffee
    dissolved in 100ml
    hot water
80g walnuts or almonds

What you do

1 **Preheat** the oven to 170°C/325°F/gas mark 3.

2 Mix flour, salt, baking powder and mixed spice in a large bowl.

3 **Whisk** the sugar and eggs together until they are thick and light-coloured.

4 Whisk in the honey, oil and coffee.

5 Add this mixture and the nuts to the flour mixture.

6 **Grease** a 20cm round cake tin with a little butter, and then pour the mixture into it. **Bake** for about 1 hour. Towards the end of that time, check that the cake is not getting too brown around the edges. If it is, turn the oven down and cover the cake with foil until it is cooked.

7 You can check if the cake is cooked by pushing a skewer or a knife into its centre. If the skewer comes out sticky, the cake is not quite done, but if it is clean, the cake is ready to come out of the oven.

8 Let the cake **cool** in its tin for about 15 minutes, and then turn it out on to a cake rack to cool completely.

Burfi (India)

Divali – the Hindu festival of light – takes place in the autumn. People decorate their homes and the streets with lights, have firework displays and share a family celebration. Indian-style sweets – called *burfi* – are a favourite at Hindu festivals. This is a simple recipe for coconut *burfi*.

What you need

200g creamed coconut
40g butter
1 tsp cardamom powder
a few strands of saffron
    (optional)
150g caster sugar
2 tbsp flaked almonds

What you do

1 Put the creamed coconut in a bowl over a pan of water.

2 Add half the butter, cardamom, saffron and sugar.

3 Place the pan over a very low heat and allow the creamed coconut and butter to **melt**.

4 Keep this mixture over the heat for 10 minutes, stirring it all the time.

5 Melt the remaining butter in a small pan. **Grease** a shallow dish, such as a 20cm square cake tin, with a little of the butter.

6 Pour the mixture into the greased cake tin and **sprinkle** almonds over it.

7 Allow the *burfi* to **cool**, and then cut it into small pieces.

Further information

Books

Festivals of the World, Professor Martin E. Marty (ed.)
(Hodder Wayland, 2002)
Sacred Food, Elizabeth Luard (MQ Publications, 2001)

Websites

http://kid.allrecipes.com
http://www.support4learning.org.uk/shap/calend2a.htm

Conversion chart

Ingredients for recipes can be measured in two different ways. Metric measurements use grams and millilitres. Imperial measurements use ounces and fluid ounces. This book uses metric measurements. The chart here shows you how to convert measurements from metric to imperial.

SOLIDS		LIQUIDS	
METRIC	IMPERIAL	METRIC	IMPERIAL
10g	¼ oz	30ml	1 fl oz
15g	½ oz	50ml	2 fl oz
25g	1 oz	75ml	2½ fl oz
50g	1¾ oz	100ml	3½ fl oz
75g	2¾ oz	125ml	4 fl oz
100g	3½ oz	150ml	5 fl oz
150g	5 oz	300ml	10 fl oz
250g	9 oz	600ml	20 fl oz
450g	1lb	900ml	30 fl oz

Healthy eating

This diagram shows you what foods you should eat to stay healthy. Most of your food should come from the bottom of the pyramid. Eat some of the foods from the middle every day. Only eat a little of the foods from the top.

Healthy eating at festival time

Festival foods are made to be eaten on very special occasions. Many of the recipes contain large quantities of sugar and fat. You should take care not to eat too much of these foods at one time, or to make them too often.

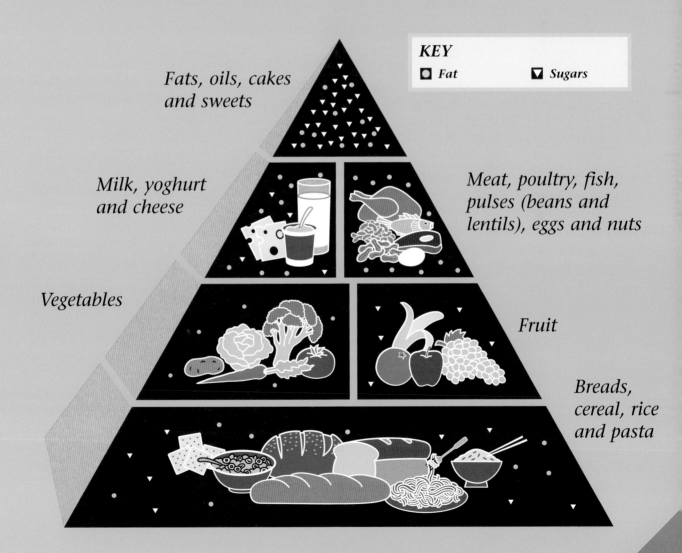

Fats, oils, cakes and sweets

KEY
◻ *Fat* ▼ *Sugars*

Milk, yoghurt and cheese

Meat, poultry, fish, pulses (beans and lentils), eggs and nuts

Vegetables

Fruit

Breads, cereal, rice and pasta

Glossary

absorb soak up

bake cook something, such as cakes or pies, in the oven

baking parchment paper with a non-stick surface that can be used to line baking trays or cake tins

baste spoon fat or oil over food to stop it drying out

batter a beaten mixture of flour, eggs and milk, for instance, that is used for making pancakes

beat mix something together strongly, using a fork, spoon or whisk

boil cook a liquid on the hob (or the flat top part of the cooker). Boiling liquid bubbles and steams strongly.

chop cut something into pieces, using a knife

colander bowl-shaped container with holes in it, used for straining vegetables and draining

cool allow hot food to become cold. You should always allow food to cool before putting it in the fridge.

dough a soft mixture that sticks together and can be shaped or rolled out – not too wet to handle, but not dry either

drain allow liquid to run out or away. A draining spoon is a large spoon with holes in its bowl.

extract flavouring, such as vanilla or almond extract. It is not the same as essence, which is much stronger.

fish slice utensil for lifting fish or other fried food out of a pan. It is like a flat spoon with slits in it.

fry cook something in oil in a pan

glaze coat food with liquid, such as a mixture of milk and egg; used to make top of bread or buns glossy during baking

grate cut into small pieces, using a grater (a kitchen utensil with lots of small holes)

grease rub fat over a surface to stop food sticking to it

knead keep pressing and pushing dough with your hands so that it becomes very soft and stretchy

melt change from solid to liquid when heated

mince squash and chop something so that it becomes a paste

ovenproof will not be cracked by the heat of an oven

paste thick mixture

peel remove the skin of a fruit or vegetable; or the skin itself (also known as rind or zest)

preheat turn the oven or grill on in advance, so that it is hot when you are ready to heat food

purée mash, sieve or blend food until it is smooth; or the blended food itself

rinse wash under a cold tap

season give extra flavour to food by adding salt or pepper

shortcrust kind of pastry with a cooked texture like a biscuit

sift shake flour or other powder through a sieve

simmer boil gently

slice cut something into thin, flat pieces

soy sauce sauce made from fermented soy beans. A popular ingredient in Chinese cooking.

sprinkle scatter small pieces or drops on to something

steam cook in steam from boiling water

stigma part of the inside of a flower that picks up pollen. Once pollen is collected on a plant's stigma, the plant can form a seed.

tender soft, but not squashy

tepid only slightly warm, lukewarm

well dip made in the centre of flour in a bowl, into which you may pour water, milk or eggs

whisk beat an ingredient, such as cream, to make it light and airy

yeast substance used to make bread rise

Index